Fatherhood:
You Can't Do It Over

Written by Dan Neville

Published by Dan Neville
Copyright © 2008 by Dan Neville

All rights reserved

First Printing: January 2008
First Edition Revised and Printed: May 24, 2008
Second Edition Printed: June 6, 2008
Second Edition Revised and Printed: **June 26, 2008**

ISBN 978-0-615-26128-7

Cover: Lorraine and Megan forming a heart in the backyard. St. George, Utah, May 2004
Back Page: Family photos depicting T-I-M-E.

Dedication

I would like to dedicate these writings to my parents. First, to my Mother. She devoted her entire life to the well-being and happiness of her family and to all others who entered her home. Also, to my Dad. He taught all of his children how to work and he was a good example of how to be a great Scout Leader.

Acknowledgements

I would like to express my appreciation to Janna Neville and Elise Winters Neville for many hours of editing and for their editing suggestions. I would also like to thank Janna, Brad, Lorraine, Kevin, and Megan for the great joy they have been and are now. It is a privilege to be associated with such noble children of our Heavenly Father.

Contents

	Forward	i
1	Just A Dad	1
2	Going To The Library	7
3	Will You Tutor My Children?	13
4	I Don't Want To Go On A Picnic	19
5	The Most Important Room In The House	25
6	Don't Miss A Single Game	33
7	Splitting Firewood	41
8	Will You Help Me With This?	53
9	The Rat Pack	61
10	Every Parent's Dream	69
11	Baseball Field Notes	77
12	Scouting Notes	87
13	The Two A's	97
14	The Joys Of Parenthood	101
15	Chef Dad	113
16	Beyond 50 Years	125
17	Summary	129

Forward

The basic premise for this book is to write down some family stories and pass them along to my children and any others who might be embarking on the rollercoaster ride of fatherhood/parenthood. I hope that the reader can find something beneficial in these family stories.

The following quotes summarize much of what I am trying to say in the following pages.

"Children are more influenced by sermons you act than by the sermons you preach"
David O. McKay 1955

"The greatest work you will ever do will be within the walls of your own home"
Harold B. Lee 1972

"No other success can compensate for failure in the home"
J.E. McCullough 1924
David O. McKay 1935

"It is not so much the major events as the small day-to-day decisions that map the course of our living....Our lives are, in reality, the sum total of our seemingly unimportant decisions and of our capacity to live by those decisions"
Gordon B. Hinckley 1965

"It isn't as bad as you sometimes think it is. It all works out. Don't worry. I say that to myself every morning. It will all work out! If you do your best, it will all work out. Put your trust in God, and move forward with faith and confidence in the future. The Lord will not forsake us."
Gordon B. Hinckley 2000

"Love is spelled T-I-M-E"
Unknown

There are many gospel principles relating to fatherhood, family life, developing relationships and our Heavenly Father's plan for us, which are not included in this work. Countless good books can be found on these subjects. But for my book I wanted to use everyday life stories that happened in our family and the practical lessons I learned.

This book is not a typical life history or autobiography. It is organized by topics instead of time periods. For this reason I thought it might be helpful to include a short chronological family timeline.

Forward iii

Dan A. Neville
    Born: November 18, 1957, while his family was living in Gardena, CA
    Moved to Simi Valley, CA in 1967
    Graduated from Royal High School in June 1975
    LDS mission to New York City from February 1977 to February 1979
    Met Janna Barlow January 1980

Janna L. Barlow
    Born: October 22, 1962, while her family was living in Santa Monica, CA
    Moved to La Canada, CA in 1967
    Moved to Northridge, CA in 1976
    Moved to Simi Valley, CA in 1977
    Met Dan January 1980
    Graduated from Simi Valley High School June 1980

Dan & Janna Neville
    Married: August 7, 1981 - LDS Los Angeles Temple
    Simi Valley, CA – August 1981 to August 1984
        Brad L. Neville born October 8, 1982
    Highland, UT – August 1984 to August 1986
        Lorraine D. Neville born October 1, 1984
    Solvang, CA – August 1986 to April 1990
        Kevin J. Neville born April 26, 1987
    Gig Harbor, WA – April 1990 to March 2001
        Megan C. Neville born June 6, 1990
    St George, UT – March 2001 to time of printing (January 2008)
        No children born at this location
        Brad – LDS Mission to Donetsk, Ukraine January 2002 to December 2003

> Brad – Married June 2004 – LDS Salt Lake City Temple
> Lorraine – Married December 2005 - LDS St. George Temple
> Kevin – LDS Mission to Buenos Aires, Argentina September 2006 to September 2008
> Megan – Senior at Dixie High School
> (at time of first printing, January 2008)

At age 50, I came to the realization that "you can't do it over." I did not write this book to claim that I did everything right. The truth is, I wrote it to try and hold on to the past, wishing that I had more time to try and do a better job at being a "Dad."

As I sketched out a simple timeline, I realized that, on the average, I have only used approximately two thirds of a life time and still have 25 to 30 more years to enjoy the blessings of fatherhood.

1
Just A Dad

No other success or pursuit is as important or rewarding as being a dad

I am not a writer or a psychologist. I am just a dad and now a grandpa. I have just turned 50. So why am I going to write a book, and especially a book in an area in which I do not have any formal training? For a long time, two thoughts have been rolling around in my head that have prompted me to sit down and begin this project.

The first thought I have pondered for years. Most things in this world we, mankind, get better at. We improve something or build something better than the previous version, such as in medicine, mechanics, technology, etc. Scientists and inventors take meticulous notes, lab notes or field notes, so that they and other researchers can learn from the first attempt and the second and third and so on. Eventually, a string with a can at each end turns into a small device in your pocket which you can communicate in a variety of ways with just about anybody, just about anywhere in the world.

If this idea of learning from past attempts and continual improvement is useful in so many areas, why is it that when we are beginning a family, or becoming a parent, and we need to understand all of the complex social skills that go along with that gargantuan endeavor, we all seem to be starting over at square one? The only thing anyone needs to do to become a father is to have a child. Can't we use this technique of learning from previous attempts, to help us with fatherhood and to enjoy the responsibility that comes with having children?

My second thought begins with a story. When my oldest of four children was about 9 or 10, we signed him up for the local version of youth baseball. It was a local athletic association that had organized a low-key sports program. (Real Little League was not yet available in our area.) A week or so after registration, I got a phone call and the person on the other end informed me that my son and approximately 10 or 11 other boys would not be able to play baseball this year because the association was short on coaches. The other dads and/or moms on the list had all said they were unable to coach. Unless I was able to coach, my son and these other kids would not be able to play that year. After running several excuses through my head such as, "I have never coached or even played organized baseball," and then pondering the consequences of my son and other boys not being able to play, I replied, "Well, I guess I will have to be the coach then." This coaching decision turned out to be one of the biggest blessings and most fun adventures of my life.

The following year when real Little League was available I was asked to be a coach, or as it is called in Little League, a manager. Although the previous year was a lot of fun, I decided that I had a lot more to learn about the game and about being a coach and that there were probably some good books that I could read to learn a few things. So I went to the Public Library and found a book that I think helped me in my coaching skills and, more importantly, after all these years has helped prompt me to take on this endeavor. This book I found in the library was written by a dad, a dad who had been asked to help coach and ended up coaching for 10 plus years. The book contained the things he had learned about coaching over the previous years that he thought might be helpful to other new coaches. It was.

So, my second thought is that if I can write down some of the things that I have learned about being a dad over the past few decades, then maybe some of these things can be as helpful to other new dads as that coach's experiences were to me as a new coach.

As mentioned earlier about starting at square one, part of the problem of being a dad is that unlike building a car or even coaching a team, where you can improve on the previous year, when you finish raising children, or at least at about the time they begin to leave home, everybody looks back and wonders, "How did I do? Did I do a good job? Did I work hard enough at it? Did I mostly make the right decisions?" The problem is: you can't do it over; you can't make improvements on the next model, you really only get one chance to raise your children.

One of the points that I would like to focus on is highlighted by a statement by one of the previous Presidents of the Church of Jesus Christ of Latter- day Saints. President David O. McKay quoted in a talk that, "No other success can compensate for failure in the home." I have heard this statement often and I would like to focus on it not as a condemnation, but as a goal, something to focus on. It is a reminder of what is, or should be, important to us as dads. Or may I say it like this: *No other success or pursuit is as important or rewarding as being a dad.*

All of us agree with the idea that when we look back on our lives we are not going to wish we had spent more time at work. This idea corresponds perfectly with, "No other success can compensate for failure in the home." None of us want to say, "Well, my family did okay without me," or, "My family didn't turn out the way I had hoped, but by not being at home very much, I sure became a good backhoe operator," or, "I sure have saved a lot of people money on their taxes," or any other good and worthwhile accomplishments we could make in many other areas. As dads, we have to be careful to focus on our families and be careful that we are not only focusing on our profession or our own hobbies and interests.

As I reflect back, my hope is that I can share some of the things that I have learned that may help others in their goal of having a successful family. The following thoughts and stories are the lab and field notes resulting from our little petri dish (our family) in the large laboratory called Earth life.

2
Going To The Library

Your family's life will be the sum total of your seemingly unimportant decisions

Let me begin this chapter with a quote. "It is not so much the major events as the small day-to-day decisions that map the course of our living.... Our lives are, in reality, the sum total of our seemingly unimportant decisions and of our capacity to live by those decisions." Gordon B. Hinckley, 1965.

As I begin to reflect on the little incidents that make up our family story, I need to acknowledge the workings of the Spirit. For example, in one of the previous stories where I mentioned that I went to the library to find a book, those who know me and read that probably stopped for a second and said, "What, Dan went to the library?" And they would be right to ask that question. I can't really think of another time that I have gone to the library to find a book that I would be interested in. That would be like my wife waking up one morning and saying, "I think I will go to a concrete finishing seminar today."

Even in simple little things like following through on the thought of going to the library, we can, when we need it, be directed by a more knowing power. That seemingly simple action of going to the library that day had a large impact on my future. It not only helped influence my coaching techniques and philosophy but ultimately helped me to be comfortable with and enjoy coaching. Coaching has been one of the ways I have been able to enjoy many years of family time and individual time with my children.

Of course there are other stories about when we could feel the promptings from the Holy Ghost more immediately. For example, in 1989, while living in Solvang, California, we knew that we were never going to be able to afford our own home because of the real estate prices in that area. We felt strongly that it was time to be looking for a new location to raise a family. We knew that this decision could be difficult because we had both grown up in Southern California and were already two hours away from our hometown and families. After much discussion and prayer, Janna and I decided to visit some friends in the Seattle, Washington area. We planned a four day trip to Washington over the Thanksgiving holiday in order to look at the area. We decided to rent a car and drive a different direction out of Seattle each day and see what we could find.

On day one we headed north towards Everett and beyond. It was very nice, but we had no special feelings. On day two we headed east out to Bellevue and Redmond. It was just as beautiful as the day before but no special feelings. That evening as we prepared for bed and had a prayer together, we felt good about what we were doing but again, we had no special feelings that we had found what we were looking for. The next day was Sunday and we headed south to Puyallup and Tacoma. While we were driving we felt good about the direction we were going. We knew it would be a long day as we headed south to Puyallup and Enumclaw, then west to

Tacoma and the Kitsap Peninsula. Later in the day as we left Tacoma, we headed across the Tacoma Narrows Bridge towards a town we had heard about called Gig Harbor. As we got off the highway and headed into the center of town, we both seemed to feel some kind of attraction to this beautiful setting that was once a small fishing village.

    We drove around a little and ended up finding an LDS church building. It was late afternoon by then and the parking lot was still full. We looked at each other thinking, "This little town seems too small to have two wards (congregations) in it." We drove around town and looked at the cute little shops, the waterfront and the subdivisions cut in among the trees. It was getting late. We headed north from Gig Harbor through more beautiful countryside and plenty of more reasonably priced places to live than in Southern California. We boarded a ferry in a little town called Southworth, which also had a couple of nice building lots just across from the ferry terminal. The ferry headed east across the Puget Sound and back to Seattle. We had been gone the whole day and had seen many different places that looked very nice and affordable.

    That evening during our prayers we knew that after all we had seen over the past three days that we needed to go back to Gig Harbor and really look it over. We woke up early, got on the phone and located a realtor that could spend the day with us prior to our late afternoon flight back to Southern California. We arrived in Gig Harbor, met up with the real estate agent and madly drove all around Gig Harbor in all directions.

After a few hours we asked him to take us to a part of town that we had briefly seen the previous day as we were headed out of town to catch the ferry. He tried to discourage us from getting too serious about "that side of town." He told us that there were other, more convenient places to look at. We felt strongly that we should look in this one particular neighborhood so he reluctantly took us there. We found a building lot there that we knew was perfect for us and also another little house that ended up being available for rent that we could move into while we built on the lot just down the street. We made an offer on that lot and also signed papers on two other lots across town that we planned to build homes on that would be for sale.

At about 2 p.m. we rushed to the airport, turned in the rental car, jumped on the plane and upon take-off we looked at each other and said, "Well, I guess we are moving to Gig Harbor." We laid our heads back for the flight, feeling calm and peaceful about the whirlwind of events that had just taken place. Within a few months, we moved to Gig Harbor and although we felt all of the typical stresses of moving, we experienced many little events that further solidified our knowledge that we had been directed by divine guidance to a little place called Gig Harbor out on the Peninsula, across the Narrows Bridge, west of Tacoma, Washington.

In this story and every other story in my book, I want to acknowledge the direction of our Heavenly Father through the Holy Ghost. Let's be clear: I was not and am not smart enough to think out ahead of time the benefits and the consequences that all of our decisions would have to our family as the years came and went. But I did try to rely on the Spirit to help me make these decisions. May I paraphrase the previous quote by Gordon B. Hinckley? *Your family's life will be the sum total of **your** seemingly unimportant decisions.*

3
Will You Tutor My Children?

The purpose of this book is to focus on the fatherhood years. Maybe a little background and a few short stories leading up to marriage and fatherhood are appropriate. I spent my early years, until the middle of 5th grade, just outside of Los Angeles, California, in the city of Gardena. At age 10, my family moved to suburbia, Simi Valley, California and we had everything a boy needed to be happy. Our Mom made us breakfast and a sack lunch everyday before school and chocolate chip cookies almost everyday after school. We had a regular home cooked meal every night, although it usually included milk that was mixed with half powdered milk to help stretch the budget. Looking back I guess Mom felt like she had to do something thrifty with eight children, a foster child, and a friend or two at the dinner table every night. We had orange groves to shoot BB guns and to have orange fights, fields with trails to ride mini bikes and motorcycles, and hills to hunt rabbits. You could ride your bicycle anywhere without having to worry about riding through the bad part of town, like in Gardena.

    Our family grew and ended up consisting of my two older brothers, me, three younger sisters, another brother, and a baby sister, Mom and Dad and miscellaneous foster children. On Monday nights my parents tried to hold Family Home Evening in earnest and they were mostly successful. I may not be able to remember the exact lessons taught, but I still remember the time together and many of the games we played. During my junior high school years, my brother David and I were in the 4-H club and we each raised a steer each of those three years to take to the Ventura County Fair and the auction. I began wrestling in seventh grade and continued wrestling through high school. I attended early morning seminary until the middle of my junior year. At that time, because I was always losing weight for wrestling, my life consisted of no or minimal breakfast, running before school, running during lunch break, regular practice in a 98 degree wrestling room after school, and a minimal dinner. My body craved food and sleep, but since sleep was the only thing enjoyable to me at the time that was allowed, early morning Seminary eventually fell by the wayside.

At age 16, and when I wasn't wrestling, I worked at a Texaco gas station in town. I drove an ugly car, a '62 Dodge Lancer GT, and graduated in 1975. At age 19, I went on a mission for the Church of Jesus Christ of Latter-day Saints to the New York, New York City Mission from Feb. 5, 1977 to Feb. 10, 1979. I began dating Janna in about January of 1980 while she was a senior in high school. (Holy mackerel)

Here is a short story that sums up my thoughts and counsel on dating, or at least about dating when you are at the age where you think you could get married. In January, 1980, when I met Janna, I was 22, and was at the age that I thought that marriage could be a year or so away. Janna was 17 and she didn't figure that marriage was in her future for many years to come. Janna asked me out on our first date and it was a lot of fun, so much fun that we must have seen each other at least 3 times a week, until late at night, from that point on. Don't get me wrong, there were plenty of ups and downs in our relationship, she was only 17, but mostly the time we spent together was great and what I thought was really fun was that she liked to go places that I wouldn't have thought of going on my own, or that I would have ever gone with the typical girl.

For instance, on one particular date we went to the J. Paul Getty Museum. The original museum was about an hour from Simi Valley, where we lived, and along the coast in the Malibu area. The museum was a former residence of the rich oil mogul and was a magnificent old house. We must have spent a good two hours walking through the oversized rooms with large fireplaces and priceless art and hallways full of intricate, hanging tapestries. I remember being impressed with her knowledge of interesting facts about some of the artwork and things, but like me she was also interested in the architecture, construction of the building, floor plan, and design. I don't think she was as interested in the details of the highly precise climate control and specialized lighting that was used to help preserve the art and bright colors of the tapestries. But at least it made her smile that it was interesting to me. We had a great time being together, and our backgrounds and interests complemented each other to enhance the experience for both of us.

As we left the museum and were about to get into my rag top Fiat Spider, (which was probably one of the reasons she went out with me in the first place) I said, "Janna, even if we don't get married, I wonder if it will be possible for you to tutor my children?" This could have been an awkward moment, it was early in our relationship, and she was not even remotely thinking of marriage, but she must have understood the meaning of the compliment because she didn't freak out and she didn't make me take her immediately home and we continued to see each other after. My point is when you are dating, look to the future, look for complimenting interests and intelligent qualities and try to have uplifting experiences that improve your confidence in yourself, your life and your future.

An interesting side note: For some reason while I was dating Janna, I signed up for a subscription to Time Magazine. It came in very handy in keeping me up to date on diverse subjects that I could use during our conversations. I think she was impressed and I felt smarter.

Once you feel like you may have found the right girl, now you may have to get her parents on your side. As Janna and I began to date regularly, her parents were concerned that she was too young to be dating, possibly falling in love and making marriage plans with an older guy. Janna had a scholarship to BYU and they were anxious for her to take advantage of that opportunity. One Sunday afternoon while Janna and I were conversing in the dining room of her home her mother, Joan, began to prepare the Sunday meal. She put out on the countertop at least 10 large potatoes and began to peel them. Janna was the oldest of 7 children and we both went in to help with dinner. Because I myself came from a large family and I had plenty of experience peeling potatoes, I asked if I could help with the dinner preparations. Joan replied, "No, no, I got it." I'm sure she was thinking that she was in a hurry and couldn't wait on me to fumble around and finally get all of those potatoes peeled. I tried to convince her that I could handle it. When she wouldn't be persuaded, I challenged her to a potato peeling race. With that suggestion, a big smile came to her face and the challenge was accepted. We selected two large equal sized potatoes and got in position in front of the sink, for the race. The rule was the first one to completely peel the potato satisfactorily for boiling would be the winner. If I won, I could help finish peeling the rest of the potatoes.

Janna yelled "Go", and we began to peel. Elbows and peels were flying everywhere. I saw Joan glance at my potato just before she elbowed me in the ribs to slow me down. Laughing, we both reached our potatoes towards the rinse water.

Both potatoes were declared ready for the pot, and the race was called a tie. With the tie, Joan consented to let me complete the pile of potatoes. From that day forth I was on the road to qualifying for her daughter.

4
I Don't Want To Go On A Picnic

If you will lose yourself in the well being of your family your joy will be endless

Trying to keep the chapters in chronological order, writing about being a young married would be next. The problem is I didn't know anything. I'm not sure I can write about something in which I had no clue. But, I guess that is why I am writing some of the things I remember, in the hope that some of my notes of the past will be of some benefit to others.   As I look back it surprises me that I did anything correctly.   For example, one beautiful Saturday morning in Southern California, after being married for about six months or so, (you know after some of the romance wears off) Janna said to me, "Let's do something fun today. Let's make a lunch and go have a picnic."

Let me stop there for a moment and give some background. Janna was working full-time in a private hospital as a receptionist, a few blocks from our apartment. In other words, she was in an office all day. I was working on a concrete and framing crew building homes. In other words, I was outside all day. Our project at the time was about a 45 minute drive away in the foothills of the California coastal range north of Malibu. It wasn't very close to any places to eat and to help save money, most days I brought a sack lunch. Our apartment was a one bedroom little place with not much of a yard, not even a common area of any kind.

Okay, back to the story. When Janna asked me to take her on a picnic, I was laying in bed or maybe I was up and laying on the couch, and without thinking clearly I said something like, "I don't want to go on a picnic. I have a picnic everyday." If I had stopped and thought more carefully for just a minute, I would have seen her idea as a good way for her to get out and enjoy the out-of-doors and for us to be together. Instead I only saw the situation from my own viewpoint which, as I recall, was met with some discussion and a few tears. In the end we did go and have a picnic and had a wonderful time together.

Another story that illustrates the intricacies of relationship adjustment happened our first New Year's Eve as newlyweds. Janna remembers this story better than I do. I know this because she brings it up every year on New Year's Eve. This particular time at work we were putting in long days working on the foundation of a large hillside home and New Year's Eve day was no exception. Our crew poured out several truckloads of concrete and hustled all day long. Janna and I had made plans to meet some friends and go to dinner and a dance, just like we used to when we were dating. After coming home a little late, almost 7:00 pm, I went into our room to get cleaned up and ready to go out. The story goes, and this is the part I don't remember, that when Janna came in to check and see if I was ready for the evening's festivities, I was asleep across the bed with the shower running. Her feelings were hurt, but she left me there to sleep hoping that I would wake up in time for some sort of celebration at midnight. Apparently I didn't wake up, at least not enough to celebrate in any fashion. I guess it wasn't a deal breaker because we are still together.

The point is that I had to learn to think of other people's feelings, especially my new wife's feelings. The picnic incident taught me that newlywed women are extremely sensitive. I needed to listen to not only what my wife was saying, I also needed to understand the feelings she was expressing. The New Year's Eve story taught me that sometimes you just can't do it all, but if you have been kind a hundred other times, you can get away with falling asleep on a big night.

Another story that I remember about those early years of marriage happened a couple of years later. After being in Simi Valley working and trying to figure out what we or I was going to do as far as a profession, we moved to Highland, Utah. At the time of the move our oldest child, Brad, was almost two years old and Janna was seven months' pregnant with our next child. We moved into a home that was owned by Janna's dad. The home needed to have the yard put in and the basement finished, all of which we would trade for rent while I attended BYU.

One Christmas, after a year-and-a-half of school, we went back to Simi Valley to spend the holidays with our families. While there, we were out Christmas shopping and I ran into my good friend's dad, Dr. Keith Baker. I had spent a lot of time at the Baker home as a youth and young adult. His son David and I were almost inseparable in junior high and high school. Almost every night I ate dinner at his house or he ate at mine, and sometimes we would eat dinner at both houses in the same night. As an older teen I dated at least two of Dr. Baker's daughters.

Being genuinely interested, he asked me what was going on in mine and Janna's life. I explained that we had two children; I was attending BYU in the Engineering program; I was working as much as I could for a General Contractor in order to buy books, gas, and groceries; I was finishing the basement of the home I was in; and I was trying to do homework in the evenings after spending some time with the family. He kind of smiled, probably trying not to laugh out loud and hurt my feelings and then he said, "I remember those days, and I think it is so important for all young families to have that wonderful experience." I have thought about that statement many times since. At the time I don't think I thought of my experience as all that wonderful. But he was right; it was a wonderful experience. All young families should be so lucky as to work hard and struggle together. The lesson to learn is that life will be full of hard times. Learn that lesson early and keep moving ahead. Do whatever it takes to get through together. This too, shall pass. It may be that the outcome will be different than you had planned or expected, and that is probably okay. One of Janna's favorite sayings is; "Heavenly Father can't steer you on the path you should go, if you are not moving forward."

This time of getting married and starting a family is where real life begins. Many young couples, especially after their first child, when the nights are long and the days even longer, may begin to question what has happened. There is no time or energy for doing the things that used to be fun. Remember, this is what you have been looking forward to, and for good reason. It may be hard to imagine, but believe me; you are going to wish this time of raising young children had not gone by so fast. The everyday struggles are always going to be there, but this is where real life begins, as you lose yourself in the well-being of your family.

This reminds me of a young married couple I heard about that was expecting their first child. A female co-worker asked the husband if they planned on breastfeeding the baby. He replied, "No, that's gross! And don't give me a big lecture about it."

The co-worker simply responded by saying, "Don't think only of yourself. Try to remember what a woman's body is specifically designed for." This young married guy's response is a good example of how self-centered men can be sometimes. *If you will lose yourself in the well being of your family, your joy will be endless.*

This is your life! Enjoy it now! I remember as a young couple, Janna and I had to help remind each other to enjoy the moment, don't keep looking ahead to some future time when you will be happy. It is too easy to think that, "I will be happy when we get a better apartment, a nicer car, a better job, done with school, own our own home, the baby sleeps through the night, the second baby sleeps through the night, the kids are all in school, we get a nicer home, when Billy's off to college, when Susie gets married, etc..." Then, all of a sudden, these good times are gone. Enjoy these moments now. You will miss these times.

5
The Most Important Room In The House

This title (The Most Important Room In The House) may seem like a chapter in the wrong book, but in reality, this might be the most important chapter in terms of keeping the proper perspective towards family relations. I will talk about some ideas in landscaping and how they pertain to the importance we place on the family. Your yard, believe it or not, can be an assurance or a testament to your kids of how much you value your time together. Of course, the landscaping project itself can be a good learning and togetherness time, but the real benefits of your yard live on much longer than the time it takes to install sprinklers or plant grass.

It took several years before we had our own yard in which to make major landscape decisions and that is okay because while the kids are small, a swing set or a play toy and your time are all that is needed. Even a nearby park can be sufficient for those early years. But after building and living in our first owned home, I learned a lesson that I consider valuable. Our first home was fairly typical; we put in the front yard as soon as construction was complete. Then as time and money became available, we completed portions of the back and side yards, one small area at a time. We always had a yard project in progress until the whole yard was completed. I think we read about that method in a home and garden type magazine and it worked just fine for getting a nice yard in on somewhat of a schedule and a budget.

    A few years later, when we built our second home, I somehow came to a new realization that has become my motto for landscaping: "The backyard is the most important room in the house." This didn't come to me through a magazine. This came by way of a distinct impression. Now, of course, in order to get along with the neighbors and to maximize the look and value of your home and also because some neighborhood covenants require it, you will probably have to put in your front yard first. But, don't spend your whole budget in the front. Do whatever it may take to get a start on the backyard. Do not spend all of your time, effort and money on the front and then quit. You can always add some more trees and shrubs later if you need to. Start right away on the backyard. What I am saying is, the front yard is not as important as the back. Why? Ask yourself this question: How much time will you spend playing with your kids in the backyard if it is nothing but dirt and weeds? The thing about kids is that they will have fun in a dirt backyard. In fact, a big pile of dirt can be one of the most fun things in the world to children. But how much time will you spend with them and their dirt pile? The answer is that if the backyard is just dirt and weeds, you will probably just keep the blinds closed and try not to think about the big mess out there.

    Now, close your eyes and envision a place to relax in the sun, or jump on a trampoline, or play in the sprinklers, or throw a ball, or have a BBQ and a picnic on the lawn, or grow a little garden, or have wiffle ball batting practice, or look up at the stars, or play badminton, or shoot some hoops, or play football in the rain, or hunt for Easter eggs, or build a human pyramid, or make a whirlpool in the wading pool or ...... the list can go on. All of these things, and more, should and can be done in your own backyard. This list isn't just for the kids; all of these activities are some of the most fun things that I have ever done. How nice it is to have a place, a yard, where the kids want to be, and where I want to be, a yard my kids and I worked on together. So, do what you have to do to the front yard: put it in yourself or have a landscaper put it in for you; it doesn't matter. But the backyard needs more thought and planning and it needs to be done as soon as possible. I'm not saying more money, I'm saying more attention. I'm saying more grass, less gravel.

    Here are some examples of things that we did and enjoyed over the years. As previously mentioned, the second home we built is where our landscape design ideas changed. This is probably partially due to our changing family dynamic; we then had four kids; Brad 11, Lorraine 9, Kevin 6, and Megan 4. This home was built on a very tight budget and followed the idea of starting small and adding on or completing things as we could afford them and while life kept moving forward. The exterior of the home was mostly completed and the front lawn was seeded. We decided that the next project would be the backyard basketball court.

One summer day we were contemplating taking our little stash of saved money and going down to California to visit the Grandparents and maybe go to Disneyland or something. I asked Janna what she would rather do with our week off, go to California, put the backyard in, or work on the kitchen. We stayed home and started our next phase of the backyard. The budget was tight, so instead of quickly getting an area mostly flat and pouring a nice 4 inch concrete pad, we tried something more cost effective. We, the boys and I, spent a lot of extra time to level and compact a 20' by 20' area in which we laid 12"x12" concrete pavers. We also added some boulders along one side for sitting. After Brad and Kevin grouted all the joints between the pavers, the area turned out very nice and doubled as our basketball court and back patio. With the addition of the free standing hoop and backboard, which had been previously used on our gravel parking area, the court was ready for use. Young boys love dirt, tools, and projects. Working together on a project is fun and important.

    Over the next few years we played several different versions of hoops from Around the World to Pig and one game we affectionately named Deathball, which also involved the trampoline. It is important to interject here that although we had the vague shape of a kitchen, and it functioned to keep us nourished, it was by no means a regular kitchen as you would know one. In other words, the basketball court was completed before the kitchen. The back lawn and side lawns were planted as soon as possible. Work continued on the home and yards, and I think the kitchen was completed or mostly completed prior to the construction of the batting cage. I cannot count the number of games of stickball, football in the rain, or pickle that were played on our lawn areas.

We constructed a batting cage from 4x4 lumber that I reclaimed from the throwaway pile of a construction project I was working on. The netting for the cage came from a golf course I drove by that was replacing all of the netting on the driving range. The batting cage was a lot of fun and very useful. Many afternoons during baseball season we had all or a portion of one of our boy's teams over for batting practice. Brad and I even developed a way to play a complete game of one-on-one baseball that we could play in the cage.

While constructing a new home in St. George, Utah, we still placed a high priority on the backyard. The backyard and front yard lawn areas were prepared and planted at the same time. The lawn areas were designed with some interesting, oversized mounds. Although hard to mow, these mounds gave depth and contour to the landscape, but mostly they were added for the purpose of sitting on, rolling down, and the occasional bike jumping. Shortly after planting the lawns, a pitcher's mound and backstop were constructed in the backyard. Kevin and I even contemplated incorporating a mountain bike trail into the landscape that would circle the house and would have various boulder obstacles and jumps. The bike trail has not been built, mainly because there are many popular mountain biking trails close by the St. George area. As with previous homes, there were always small landscaping projects to do or finish. Many trees and plants were added over the years for adult enjoyment. Even thought the landscaping continued, shortly after moving into our home, Megan and I were able to play and did play many a badminton game in our backyard.

In conclusion, don't put off or miss out on the quality fun times that can be had in your properly designed backyard. Remember to have a simple, practical, usable design. You can do it yourself. You don't have to spend a lot of money, just time and thought. Have the kids help if you can. They aren't going to be interested in helping plant a bunch of trees or spreading a ton of gravel, but they will enjoy helping build a playhouse, or a pitcher's mound, or a soccer goal, or a sandbox, or a swing set or a basketball court, or a .... again, the list goes on and on. Just remember, with proper thought the backyard can be both beautiful and useable, and a source of many fond memories.

6
Don't Miss A Single Game

I arose early one Saturday morning about a year or so after moving to Gig Harbor. I needed to complete a chore prior to Brad's mid-morning basketball game. Brad was in the 5th grade and this was his first season in the sport of basketball. We enjoyed going to his games and supporting him. I had become the owner of a small cabin cruiser boat (more on the boat in the Don'ts Chapter) (If I write one). This boat was just large enough that I wasn't able to pull it around on a trailer (which I didn't have anyway). It was moored to a buoy near a friend's home in the Raft Island Harbor, on the other side of town from where we lived. The buoy and weight I had constructed to moor the boat were not sufficient enough for the high winter winds. The winds forced the boat to drag the weight around and it had been moving somewhat harmlessly about the little harbor. After a big storm, it eventually broke completely free from the buoy and some neighbors and friends had rescued the boat and temporarily secured it to another buoy. It was urgent that I take care of the boat and move it to safety as soon as possible.

The plan was to drive across town, paddle a little inflatable boat out to the big boat, hopefully get it started and then motor it around the Peninsula to our side of town and into the more protected harbor that was Gig Harbor proper. I figured that I could anchor the boat there for the following week until I could fabricate a new and much stronger buoy. I had planned to anchor the boat out from but near to the public boat ramp, paddle the little inflatable to shore about the same time Janna was heading out to the game, she could pick me up and we would all watch Brad's game together. After the game, we could go pick up my vehicle on the other side of town.

As is typical with boats, things do not always go as smoothly and as timely as you have planned. I can remember coming around the south end of Point Fosdick and heading north underneath the Tacoma Narrows Bridge. I realized that the rendezvous time had passed and that Janna would be headed to the game with Brad and the other kids to be on time for warm-ups. Try to remember, these were the days when personal cell phones were not yet in everyone's pocket, or even on the market. Motoring slowly through the narrow opening of the Harbor, I decided I would head towards the public boat dock, which was located on the west side of the harbor or the town side, instead of the public ramp which was located on the opposite side of the harbor, in the hope that there would be a pay phone available, although I wasn't sure who I would call. So, that is what I did.

After I secured the boat to the dock, I walked up the ramp towards town. I located a pay phone and decided to try our home phone just in case. While listening to the rings I noticed a bench and a pole not too far from where I was. The pole looked like it had a bus schedule on it. As I expected, the rings went unanswered. So I hung up the phone and went to see if, by any chance, a bus would be coming by soon and where it might be headed. I had not ridden a city bus since my mission in New York City, but it seemed like a good option.

As near as I could decipher, it looked as though a bus would be by in about 10 minutes and would be headed north along Harborview continuing north on Peacock Hill and then west on 144th continuing out to the Key Peninsula. Wow, this seemed to be the perfect solution! The school where the game was to be played was just a few blocks south of 144th street at Purdy Elementary. I ran back to double-check the boat and its moorings and then returned to the bus stop area just as the bus was pulling up. I verified with the driver that the bus was indeed headed where I had thought. Not being a seasoned bus rider, I sat down near the driver and explained where I was going. He said, "No problem, I'll get you close." After about a 5 mile bus ride he pulled over to the side of the road (not at a usual stop) on 144th. I got out, waited for the bus to pull away and then crossed the street and began my 2-3 block jog to the school. I walked in and sat down next to Janna just prior to the tip off.

I don't remember exactly when, but sometime during that morning I had this simple thought: "Don't miss a single game" and during the eleven years we lived in Gig Harbor, I didn't. Later on, when all four kids were playing baseball, we had to split up a couple of times. But one of us was always there and I always made an effort to be at every game, if possible. It wasn't easy, but that was what I wanted to do, so I made it happen.

Over the years, I can remember other close calls or long distances that had to be driven. For example, driving 4 ½ hours from St. George to Tooele to watch a 1 hour basketball game. But it was a goal I had and I believe it was an inspired goal. Usually without too much difficulty, schedules could be arranged and preparations could be made so that all games could be attended. Later, for the first few years after moving to St. George, I worked out-of-state. I had to modify my goal (for a short time) to attend at least all games that were on Friday nights and Saturdays.

On one occasion I remember modifying my flight schedule so as to try to attend a Friday afternoon basketball game of Kevin's. I recall returning home from Texas, flying into Las Vegas, running out of the airport (most people were running in), out to the parking structure, and then driving a little faster than normal to get to a game in Mesquite, Nevada.

During Brad's high school years, he was on the wrestling team and the baseball team. During his freshman year he also played the saxophone and was a member of the Jazz Band and Pep Band. Not only did we attend all of his baseball games, wrestling meets and tournaments, we also attended many football and basketball games in which the Pep Band was playing. Later on, when Lorraine was a cheerleader, we attended many more football and basketball games so that we could be a part of her activities. Eventually we were attending baseball, softball, football, and soccer games, talent shows, plays, spelling bees, concerts, and scouting events. We usually encouraged the rest of the kids to come and support each other as well.

As was previously mentioned, I became a baseball coach and shortly after that I became a Scoutmaster. I will have more on coaching and some scouting stories in chapters to follow. But, as you can imagine, for eight years during the Spring, it was difficult to coordinate Scout campouts and baseball schedules. But somehow we made it work and we had many wonderful experiences. It took a lot of planning, scheduling and driving but it was worth it.

One of my many fond memories was the two years I was able to coach both Lorraine and Kevin on the same Little League baseball team, the Red Birds. It was a Triple A Minor League team. When they started, Lorraine was 11 and Kevin was 9. We had a lot of fun those two years. I coached, Janna was President of the League and almost all of our kids played. One week, in the middle of the season, the other coaches and parents called a special meeting with the Gig Harbor Little League President, Janna Neville, to complain that Coach Neville and the Red Birds were playing too aggressively.

My Assistant Coach, Tenny "send 'em" Stenerodden and I had to explain our coaching philosophy that babying these kids wasn't going to help them progress or have them ready to play up in the Little League Majors. We won out; no sanctions or new rules were made. Lorraine didn't mind the aggressive play at all. One of the things she enjoyed most, when she wasn't leading a cheer from the dugout, was stealing home. We were the American League Champions those two years. From there, Lorraine went on to play girls' fast pitch softball and Kevin moved up to the Majors. I could probably go on forever with stories of games: games we should have won, games we won with miracle home runs, All-star games, Championship games, hikes, mountain climbs, rafting trips, Eagle Scout awards.

Yes, your kids will remember the time you spent with them. They will have many fond memories of games and outings and events. But just as importantly, you will have those same memories. You were there too, being just as involved. Of course you don't have to be a Little League coach or a Scoutmaster to be involved with your kids. Show support at games, play catch in the yard, attend Scout outings and other events. As I look back, these are just some of the blessings and opportunities that somehow came my way, that allowed me to be involved with my family and create bonds that are lasting and hopefully unbreakable. I look forward to these bonds lasting beyond the time when my children leave home and far into the future. I look forward to many more fun family times and outings.

I began this chapter with a story that involved our oldest son Brad and me as I tried not to miss a basketball game. Let me conclude with a short story about a neighbor boy who was about Brad's same age. Upon moving to Gig Harbor, Washington we had found and moved into a little rental home while we built a home just down the street. Across the street from our rental home, in our cul-de-sac, lived a boy who we will call Johnny. Brad and Johnny became friends and spent a lot of time together riding bikes and doing other general after school activities. While I was framing our house they would often come down the street to climb around on what must have seemed like the world's largest play toy. I could usually get them to help with a small project of some kind, and then they were off down the jogging trail on their bikes.

Johnny was the only child at home and both of his parents worked. His father seemed to return home from work in the evening at about 6:00 or 7:00 PM. His mother would leave for work prior to Johnny getting home from school. Because Johnny was often home alone in the evening, we had him over for dinner a lot and he was always invited to accompany our family on any activity or trip into town. On these occasions Johnny would run home to call his mom or dad to let them know where he would be. Later we learned that every day after work for a few hours Johnny's dad would go to the bar where his mom worked. I guess it was convenient that Johnny could get a hold of both of his parents at the same place. After moving out of the cul-de-sac, we did not see much of Johnny any more and we completely lost track of him a year or so later when we moved out of the neighborhood. I can only hope that things worked out for him.

7
Splitting Firewood

All punishment should be positive

Darkness comes early during the winter in the Northwest and is usually accompanied by drizzle or rain. At the end of December and early January it got dark about 4:30 PM at our little home tucked away in the woods near Crescent Lake. Our Crescent Lake home had a wonderful old wood burning stove in the basement family room and a beautiful rock fireplace upstairs in the living room. Both of these brought much joy, warmth and harmony to our home during those short, mostly gray days and the long wet nights. You might ask why harmony? That's a strange word to describe a fireplace. Long winter nights can be a little gloomy especially for young kids and young teens. It was always a struggle to keep everyone happy, harmonious and under control during those short afternoons and long damp evenings with not much time for outdoor activities and most of the time during these months spent indoors. Lucky Mom!

By the time I would get home in the evenings, the homework had been forcefully completed and the roughhousing was just getting started. Dinner would be ready just in time to interrupt the activities and delay the inevitable: somebody getting hurt and crying. After dinner the activities would usually include getting a nice fire going in the living room fireplace and stoking up the woodstove downstairs. We had electric heaters, but we enjoyed the crackling fires in the evening and we had an unlimited supply of firewood.

Once the after-dinner chores were done, things would get back to normal and the roughhousing would resume, with some teasing thrown in. It wouldn't be too long before one of the kids (usually one of the girls) was crying. Brad or Kevin would get the blame, and it didn't really matter which one was to blame because the punishment was the same. "Go out and split some wood," I would say. The boys would look dejected, put on shoes and coats, and grab a flashlight. Then they'd head out to the shed where there was a never-ending supply of log rounds that needed to be split for use in our nice glowing fireplaces.

It was nice. No yelling had to take place. No sending them to their room where grumbling about whose fault it was could be heard by all. Excess energy was expended and a new bundle of split wood was stacked on the back porch. The girls had some time to relax and the boys would come in usually laughing and happy.

Sometimes too happy. I would find out later that the boys, even while working, were goofing off. When this remedy for excess roughhousing first started, Kevin was too small to lift the axe and was unable to split the logs, so his job was to hold the flashlight and to point it at the proper location on the up-turned round of wood. Well it turns out that Kevin's favorite trick was to shut off the flashlight just as Brad was about to begin his downward swing. Later, with some strong counsel on the seriousness and danger of goofing off while using sharp tools, the boys got really good at splitting wood and we always had a nice big supply on our back porch.

I quickly learned, after stumbling onto this method of reform, that all punishments should somehow have a positive accomplishment attached to them. When the boys would look at the large pile of wood in the yard, they were proud of it. There wasn't anything negative associated with it. They often commented, "Look at all that wood we split!" Never did I hear a complaint or a negative remark like, "Look at all that wood you made us split."

I learned from this to modify all punishments to be positive and have an ending. If somebody was grounded for something, they must accomplish a task or goal. For instance, a new book read, or a thousand free throws shot, or a Scouting Merit Badge completed, etc. I wanted all punishments to have an ending with a positive outcome, becoming a tool and not a barrier. When these good things were completed, the grounding was over.

The above story and resulting thoughts on punishment were emphasized by this: "The rest of the story." One morning as I was headed to work at about daylight, I came up to a stop sign at a rural three way intersection. Across the street I saw an older lady dragging some branches along the side of the road and then she turned into the driveway of an older home. I saw a smokeless chimney coming from the roof at the center of the home. I concluded that the home's source of heat must have been a centrally located wood or coal burning stove. As I passed on by I didn't see a stack of firewood or pile of coal. The branches and sticks she'd been dragging must have been collected for a little morning fire. I picked up my cell phone and called home to talk to Brad. (Wait a minute, it doesn't seem like cell phones and twigs for warmth fit together in the same story.) I said, "Brad I have a little project for you. Will you and Kevin load up your truck with as much of your nicely split wood as will fit and before you leave for school, take it to this lady who I think could use it?" I explained what I had seen and the location of the house. He said he would. I was happy upon returning from work that evening to see smoke coming from her chimney and a nicely stacked pile of firewood near her back door. I was also happy to learn from Janna how quickly the boys jumped on the project and how willing they were to share and give away some of their hard work.

Years later, while sitting around the dinner table discussing Kevin's recent grounding and contemplating options, Janna came up with a solution for Kevin to have a positive experience and thus end his predicament. She suggested that the grounding could end if he would call a certain girl, (who shall remain nameless, but was a friend of Kevin's) and formally take her out on a real date. You should have heard the complaining and whining, especially as Janna explained the intricacies of a formal date. "You must have a plan. You will call her to ask her. You will tell her what to expect or plan on. You will go to the door and chat with her parents and explain what you are doing, where you will be and what time you will be back. You will open all doors for her, and upon returning, you will walk her to the door and thank her for spending the evening with you. Also," she continued, "you must, on this occasion, do all of this without the help of your friends." He had to go on a real date, not just goof around with his buddies.

By the look on Kevin's face you would have thought that someone had stolen his mountain bike or something. Now, what you need to know is that Kevin was probably close to 18 years old, certainly old enough to know how to treat a girl to a real date. Under normal circumstances we would have encouraged a double date, but this time he would have to do it on his own. Kevin had plenty of excuses like: "Nobody dates like that anymore, my truck isn't working right, I don't have any money."

Janna answered with, "Well, it's time you learned how to date like that. You can use my car, and I will loan you the money." Kevin went on the date and thus fulfilled the grounding criteria.

After the date I asked him how it was. He grumbled, "It was fine."

I asked, "Did you have fun?"

He mumbled, "Yes."

"Well," I said, "Are you going to go out like that again?"

Kevin, louder this time, "No."

I was surprised, "Why not?"

"Too much work," he said as he walked away.

A few days later one of Kevin's friends came walking swiftly into the house calling, "Mrs. Neville, Mrs. Neville, now let me get this straight! Kevin gets in trouble and his punishment is that he has to ask a beautiful girl out to dinner and a movie, walk her to the door at the end of the evening and that's it? And you paid for it?"

Janna answered, "Yep."

Let me tell you another story where there was even more complaining and grumbling. During Kevin's junior year, in the middle of basketball season, Kevin was the JV point guard. The JV team was having a great season, winning most of their games. Kevin, as point guard, was leading the team on the court and in scoring also, playing just about full games without much rest. The JV coach had nothing but confidence in Kevin.

The High School basketball program was set up so that the starting JV players also suited up for the Varsity games and were the bench players. Apparently, the head coach or Varsity coach and Kevin did not see eye-to-eye. In fact, Kevin would sit on the opposite end of the bench away from the head coach and not make eye contact the whole game. This began after the first few Varsity games in which Kevin didn't get any playing time at all, not even at the end of games where the score was not close. To add insult to injury, some players who were less critical to the JV's success were getting in for Varsity playing time. There was no explanation or even a conversation from the coach.

Pre-season games came and went and the regular season was approaching the mid-point. I guess Kevin's frustration was now showing up off the court. Prior to a game right before the mid-season break, Kevin and some friends had gone to Cedar City to watch the girl's basketball team play. As they were returning, for some reason Kevin was driving (it wasn't even his car) and he proceeded to exceed the speed limit. To shorten a long story, the officer was being very nice by writing the ticket for only 95 miles an hour. Kevin came home that evening and told us about the mishap. He explained that he would quit basketball, get a job and pay for the ticket. I'm sure I said something like "That's for dang sure," and we all went to bed.

The next day was Friday and I pondered the problem throughout the work day. That evening the basketball games were at home, and they were the final games before a one game break in the schedule at mid-season. Kevin played his usual complete JV game except for an approximate two-minute rest. Kevin warmed up with the Varsity like usual and sat at the end of the bench the entire game. Only this time I could see the emotional stress in his face. This time he couldn't hide it by joking around with the other bench warmers as he had done in the previous games. As I sat there and watched and continued to contemplate the situation through the first half, I was almost in agreement with Kevin's plan to quit, but I didn't quite feel good about that plan and as the second half proceeded I began to have an idea. I just hoped that Kevin would not do anything too drastic in the locker room without further discussion.

In the previous night's discussion, Kevin had lost his driving privileges, so we waited for the boys to emerge from the locker room and we gave Kevin a ride home. The ride home was emotional; Kevin was about to explode. Kevin and Janna discussed that if basketball was going to cause this much stress and if Kevin and the coach were not going to be able to get along, then it probably was better to quit and forget about it.

    I listened quietly, still contemplating whether or not to implement my new plan. As we pulled into the driveway, I felt good about the plan and I told them what was going to happen. The plan was a simple one. Kevin was not going to quit the team, and his driving privileges would be restored as soon as he played 5 minutes of a Varsity game. He would still have to pay for the ticket but we would figure out how later. There was silence for several minutes and then I think Janna and Kevin started to say at the same time, "That might not be until next year."

    "That's right," I said, "or it could be next Friday, it is all up to you." They both complained that it also depended on (and I quote) "a crappy coach." I don't remember my response except that I felt good about the plan.

    We discussed some possible ways to help make playing happen sooner rather than later and we went in the house. For the following week I think Kevin worked as hard in basketball practice as he is now working in a little town just outside of Buenos Aries, Argentina as a missionary for the Church. The next Friday, as we sat in a rival school gym, with about 5 minutes before the Varsity game halftime, #32 jogged over and sat in front of the scorer's table. At the next whistle, Kevin went into the game. A few minutes of playing time in the first half and a few more in the second half and Kevin's driving privileges were restored and the beginning of a rollercoaster ride of Varsity basketball had begun.

Kevin was able to play more and more during the rest of that season, including several minutes of playing time in each of the state tournament games. The following season is a whole other story, but Kevin worked hard and was the Varsity point guard for his senior year, something that he almost missed out on. We were glad for the lesson that we had learned earlier, that: *All punishment should be positive.*

How does the saying go? "You can catch more flies with honey than with vinegar." Here is another angle on positive punishment. At different ages children will go through phases of not wanting to go to bed. At about age 11, our youngest daughter seemed to have real trouble in this area. As I recall, her bed time was about 9:00 p.m. Many a night our patience would be running short at about 10:00 or 10:30 as we worked through excuse after excuse. Something like the following would typically occur on these particular nights. First, an extra long time was taken in the bathroom. Then she would come out with something on her mind. Then spend some time doing something in her room. Then back out again for a drink of water. Then she had something else to discuss. Then, "My tummy hurts." Then frustration, yelling and nobody being able to go to bed happy.

Somehow on one occasion I said something like, "If you get in bed on time I will come in and give you a back massage." It was a miracle. At 9:00 p.m. all was calm, at 9:30 p.m. all was quiet, and she was asleep. Well, that became a no-brainer. On those nights where extra attention was needed, it was much easier and much more positive for Janna or I to give a 10 minute back rub than spend 30 to 60 minutes trying to explain and then yelling about why she needed to be in bed.

8
Will You Help Me With This?

As your children learn to listen to your guidance with fun things they will be more likely to listen to your guidance with important things

It was a typical Christmas Eve, the family gathered around the beautifully decorated tree. Christmas stories from the scriptures were being acted out with towels and bathrobes as costumes. Everyone was eating homemade fudge and divinity. We continued the family tradition of one gift being opened that evening. After a few last minute wrappings, we retired to bed with anticipation for the next morning.

Christmas morning this year was different than in years past. All the kids were older now and everybody slept in till at least 7:00, almost 8:00 a.m. Brad was 21 and just home from a two year mission to the Ukraine. Lorraine was 19, working and going to school. Kevin was 16 and playing basketball. And Megan was 14, a growing teenager. Everybody was excited for Christmas but valuing any extra sleep they could get. Eventually, they got out of bed, gifts were exchanged and opened and all that was left was the clean up and the Christmas meal. In the past, Christmas days would be filled with playing with the assortment of toys and games that everyone received, trying on the new clothes left under the tree and general relaxation. This Christmas was a little different. Something unusual had been left under the tree. This year, a Millermatic 135 wire welder was left by Santa Claus. Sweet!

By 10:00 a.m. the boys were saying, "Dad, come and help us in the garage." By 10:30, loud, strange noises could be heard coming from the garage. Brad was designing and preparing to cut out pieces of steel for a new rear bumper for his Bronco and Kevin had the Sawsall out and was cutting off the back end of his Toyota truck bed. It didn't seem to be the typical relaxing Christmas Day, but we were having a lot of fun.

Janna and the girls were making a big dinner and would periodically stick their heads out to see what all the racket was. By mealtime, sparks were flying from the new welder as Brad began to tack weld steel plates together. The back of Kevin's truck was lying on the garage floor. By the end of Christmas day, Brad was a professional welder (well, almost) and from the rear, Kevin's truck looked back to normal, except from the side, where you could see a vertical scar running up the rear fender just behind the wheel well and the truck bed was 12 inches shorter. We made a lot of noise and a big mess but it might have been one of our favorite Christmas memories.

Now, let's jump back several years to when Lorraine was in the fifth grade. She told me that her teacher had said that their classroom was in need of some bookshelves. Lorraine asked me if I could come to their classroom and help solve the problem by building some bookshelves in class for show and tell and then leave them there for the classroom to use. I agreed to the project. I figured this would be as close as I would get to my own TV show like "Old Yankee Workshop". I talked to the teacher and got her ideas, came up with a little plan and scheduled a day to come to her classroom.

On the appointed day, I gathered my tools and the materials that I would need. Previous to going to the classroom, I cut out most of the pieces for the project and loosely fit them together so that all would go smoothly in front of my audience. After arriving at the classroom and introducing myself, we went out of a rear door, onto the playground. I removed the material and tools from my truck and began my show, I mean show-and-tell. I cut out the remaining pieces for the project, explaining some techniques and safety precautions as I went along. I had some volunteers help spread glue and insert screws at all the appropriate locations and within about 30 minutes or so, we had a nice piece of furniture that could be displayed in the classroom and helped organize all of the books. The shelves turned out great. Lorraine was involved and knew that I cared about her, her books, and her school.

I had the privilege of coaching the 9- and 10-year-old American League All-star Team for a couple of years. On one occasion after the last game of our season, I had a mom come up to me and thank me for the time I had spent with the kids and she complimented me on my coaching style. She mentioned that she had been to many practices over the years and that she liked the way I didn't just tell the kids what they were doing wrong, and then tell them how to do it right, but that I physically showed them by example. If I was teaching sliding then I would slide and show the proper technique. If we were practicing scooping ground balls or the outfield crow hop then I would show them first. If something was done improperly, then the kids were shown the proper method, not just told they were doing it wrong. Being a little embarrassed, I thanked her very much for the wonderful compliment. As I thought about what she had said I kind of thought, "That is the way all coaches do it, isn't it?" Then I remembered that I was lucky enough to have learned this way of coaching from the example of another coach in our league.

During the preceding few years, this coach was a great example to me, even though he was our team's nemesis. First of all, this coach's team won almost all of their games, including ones against us; second, I never heard anything negative come from his direction, either to the players or the umpires. He was nothing but nice and fair when we played his team. He was always energetic and positive and I remembered that out of all the other coaches that I knew, he was the only one like that. I wanted to be like or at least coach just like Jay Wylie. After coaching Brad for three years myself, I was excited when Brad moved up to a different age group along with Coach Wylie and his son and became a part of Jay's new team.

Years later, one hot summer day, we as a family went to Sand Hollow Reservoir to go swimming and do some cliff jumping. We were swimming from exposed rock to exposed rock, climbing up on some of the taller ones with straight cliff sides and jumping. Kevin met up with one of his good friends and they went off on their own. A little while later, I climbed up on a rock and saw them standing near the edge. I yelled, "Coming through!" and ran past them off the edge of the cliff and did a back gainer into the water. For years after, Kevin's friend Nick would say something like, "Remember that cool gainer your dad did?" It was interesting to me that at the time this seemingly simple dive would have made such an impression. Those boys could and did do much better dives than that. But, I guess for an old dude it was okay.

Later, while on a boat trip or some other activity, when Kevin was contemplating jumping off of a cliff, when he got to where he thought he wanted to jump from he would ask me if I thought it was okay. It was always a little surprising that if I said I thought it was too high he would listen and come down lower. I often wished raising teenagers would be that easy, especially when faced with deciding whether or not something was okay.

Now, to connect these stories. As I ponder back over the years of my kids' lives, I ask myself, "Why, unlike so many other teenagers in the world, did my kids seem to value my opinion? Why did they almost always listen to what I had to say?" I think part of the answer is that if they grow up watching you and learning that your opinion, advice, actions or counsel about things that are fun and interesting to them are of value, and they can see that it will help them, then they will learn that your advice is given in the spirit of help.

Why would a teenager who has never seen his dad do anything fun or useful to him suddenly listen to his dad's advice when he really needed it? My kids have spent their lives watching me have fun with them and be instructive and useful to them in a lot of areas that were important to them like school, baseball, cliff jumping, building, cars, scouting, etc. My kids were perfectly willing to take my advice on how to slide properly, or how to build something, or how to weld something, or how high was too high, etc... So, when they needed help or advice in other more important matters or I felt like they needed help or advice in their later years, they were also willing to listen to Dad.

As I have mentioned before, I am grateful for the opportunity that I was given to be able to coach and be a Scoutmaster. I was also blessed with the opportunity to help them learn how to work on cars and home-improvement projects. I learned these things from my Dad. So, for example, if your kids will come to you for help or advice on fixing a car, or help with batting practice before a team tryout, or to have you repair a broken item, and they know from your actions that you know what you are doing and that you care about them, maybe later, when their opinions or ideas are different than yours, they will think twice about what you have to say. They will remember that all your counsel and help have always been for their good.

Do things with your kids that are interesting to them and you. As you give guidance and counsel in these activities, they will learn to trust in your judgment and ask for your help. *As your children learn to listen to your guidance with fun things, they will be more likely to listen to your guidance with important things.* Of course, my examples have to do with things that interested us from sports, camping, building, to working on four-wheel-drive vehicles. You will pick things that interest you and your family; it may be music, cooking, hunting and fishing or working with computers. It doesn't matter what the activity is as long as you spend time and are having fun. If you make things fun, they will enjoy the things that you enjoy.

Working together is also a great way to teach your kids important skills and develop important relationships. As a self-employed contractor I had my sons working with me as much as I could. A couple of weeks ago I got a call from my married son who lives in another state about how to wire a new three way electrical switch in his remodeled entry. We talked about it; and I drew a little schematic on the computer and emailed it to him. He looked it over and when I was down there the next time I was able to flip on the switch and see it work. Whatever your situation, there are opportunities to work alongside your children. They will understand the importance of work and they will learn to listen to your guidance.

If kids grow up learning and knowing that you can help them with the things that interest them and you're not just sitting at home or keeping busy at work and then telling them how to do things better, then you will have a greater chance of influencing them in later years.

9
The Rat Pack

Family members should be among your child's best friends

The other day I watched a family movie from the year 1995. I witnessed a scene that I could barely remember and would not have remembered if not for the video. Our four kids were in the yard playing in the fresh snow. Snow in the winter in Gig Harbor is not that rare, but it is unusual enough that when it accumulates on the ground it makes for a fun time for all. I watched the kids and me on the video playing with each other, sledding down a small hill, jumping on the trampoline covered in snow and having a snowball fight in which it looks as though I might have been the instigator. I watched them sled forming a chain. I watched them sled on top of each other. I watched them try it standing up. I watched them try it backwards. I watched them quibble a little over whose turn it was. I watched them help each other get up after a crash. The bottom line is I watched them have a lot of fun with each other and their parents. I watched them learn to not just love each other but to like each other.

It reminded me of a discussion that Janna and I have had several times in recent years, after moving to St. George and living in a more formal neighborhood again. The discussion is based on this question: Is a nice comfortable neighborhood with good friends and neighbors a positive thing? What do you mean? A nice

The Rat Pack

home in a close knit neighborhood? It's the American Dream, isn't it?

One of the biggest reasons we moved all the way from Southern California to Gig Harbor, Washington when our family was young was in pursuit of that dream. I'm not saying neighborhoods are or aren't bad, or that living in one shouldn't be the dream, but here are some observations that we have had. I need to emphasize "we," because Janna may have more concern and input on this subject than I. Of course, there are many good and wonderful things about a neighborhood, such as a next door neighbor you can borrow an egg or a cup of sugar from. Someone who will take out your trash can and feed your goldfish when you are out of town. Someone to help carpool the kids to school and other activities. Someone to share fireworks in the cul-de-sac with on the 4th of July. In other words, a neighborhood is: other people close by who are almost as interested in the well-being and safety of your family as you are.

That all sounds pretty good and it is, but there are some things to be careful of. We loved our little neighborhood in which we lived when we first moved to Gig Harbor. All of our kids were young, approximate ages, 8, 6, 3 and 1. There were plenty of kids the same age. This is where we first witnessed the phenomenon we call the Rat Pack: groups of children running from house to house to see what holds their attention.

In our attempt to keep an eye on our children, or I should say Janna's attempt to know where her children were at all times, the pack seemed to mostly be running in our front door and then out the back door in what seemed like an endless loop. Occasionally the group height would change or there might be more than one group at a time. Although annoying, it seemed like the good life. One of the very reasons you choose where you live is the hope that there are other children for your kids to play with.

A few years later we had the opportunity to build another home using the equity in our young family dream home and a lot of sweat equity to lower our monthly expenses and try to meet our goal of no house payment. I didn't think Janna would be too excited to exchange the comforts of our cozy friendly neighborhood for the solitude of a home that some may classify as out in the sticks. I'm not totally sure how she felt about the new adventure, but she did say she would be glad not to have the responsibility for the well-being of all of the neighbor's children.

As we now look back, we are grateful for the divine intervention and the blessings that came from living in a home with almost no close neighbors with children. Every neighborhood has a group of kids who run from house to house or yard to yard looking for the next fun thing to do. They laugh and play together having a lot of fun, sometimes getting into trouble, but mostly just having fun. What could be wrong with that? This turns out to be the problem. Sometimes as parents it's too easy to send the kids out to play for several hours at a time, kind of knowing where they're at and what they are doing.

For example one afternoon in St. George, while I was in the backyard tending to the food on the BBQ, a portion of the local rat pack came running between our house and my neighbor's house. After spotting me and being very nice and polite children, they came running over to see what I was up to and probably to see if there were any handouts to be had. After exchanging hellos and asking what I was cooking and then deciding the food wasn't quite ready, they began to turn in preparation to disappear in a cloud of dust.

One of the 8-year-old boys stopped, and pointing to the girl who was with them, said, "I kiss her."

Caught somewhat off guard I said, "You do?"

He replied, "Yeah, a lot."

About that time one of the other boys said, "Let's get her." She took off running. The boys followed and around the corner of the neighbor's house they went. I kept my eye on them as they circled the house a few times. The first time around she was laughing and giggling. The second time around she began to tire of the game. I stopped the boys and told them they couldn't kiss her if she didn't want them to. They stopped and all wandered over to the neighbor's trampoline and began to jump.

I went in the house and upon my next visit out to the BBQ I heard one of the boys say, "Let's wrestle and the winner gets the girl." The group consisted of four boys and one girl. Two of the boys who were slightly older than the other two were doing the girl chasing. The other two boys were just tagging along, learning from the example of the others.

I contrast that fairly innocent story with another from our "out in the sticks" home in Gig Harbor. One spring afternoon the snow began to fall, the big snow flakes seemed to lift the spirits on what seemed to have been a fairly typical, mostly cloudy day. The boys (ages 14 and 9) ran outside to shoot some baskets and to play a little one on one basketball. To further add to the excitement of playing basketball in the snow, they took their shirts off. Megan, age 7, seeing the festivities going on outside, ran out onto the porch, and wanting to fit in, took her shirt off and ran out into the action and expected to play. Without a hint of annoyance, in fact probably grateful for any amount of help against his much taller older brother, Kevin passed Megan the ball.

I don't think I thought much about it then, but now as I look back again at the blessings of the past, I can't help but think of how that scene might have been different if that scenario were played out in a more typical neighborhood. First, with nearly five years difference in age, we would have been lucky if the two boys would have been playing together. Most likely one of them would have been playing with friends his own age and the other may have felt left out. Secondly, picture a little sister who can't even throw the ball high enough to reach the rim and is not wearing a shirt. I think we can all picture the rejection which might have taken place in a regular setting and the sadness on a little girl's face.

I understand that we don't always have a choice in the exact location or surroundings of our homes. Work, finances and many other factors have to be and are considered when choosing living accommodations and locations. I also understand that we cannot and should not choose to isolate ourselves from the rest of humanity. In fact, most of us, if given the choice, would choose to enjoy the many comforts and conveniences found in our typical suburban neighborhoods. But here is a list of some things to consider.

1   Kids who have not learned to have fun with their siblings may not feel the desire to stay close to them in later years.

2   Kids who have not learned to have fun with their parents may not feel the desire to have fun and stay close with their parents in later years.

3   And vice versa, parents who have not learned to have fun with their kids will not know how to have fun with their adult children in later years.

4   Kids who have learned most of the ways of life from their friends or peers will not feel a need or even realize to ask parents for advice.

Again, I am not saying move out of your neighborhoods and isolate yourselves. Just be aware of some of the pitfalls and errors we as parents make while enjoying the perceived security of our neighborhoods. Although hard, you may want to think twice next time you kick the kids out the front door and say, "Don't come home until dinner, I am taking a nap." What I am trying to say is that in all of our different living situations, accommodations and locations, we should remember that: *Family members (including parents) should be among our children's best friends.*

10
Every Parent's Dream

Happy teenage children making good choices

A few years ago, I was asked to write down a short spiritual personal experience that I could share with others. I wrote a little story which I titled "A Moving Experience." It was a story in which I compiled our family's two major moves and our thoughts and impressions as we went through those two life-changing experiences. Our first of the two moving experiences was 1,100 miles from Southern California to Gig Harbor, Washington. I talked about this move earlier in Chapter 2, so I won't go into detail here, just suffice it to say that Janna and I had both grown up in Southern California and we liked where we were living in Solvang. We had three kids and Janna was nearly seven months pregnant with our fourth, not usually a good time to load everything you own in a trailer and hit the road. But we did it because we felt inspired to do it. The move was a great blessing to us and our family.

Our second moving and life-changing experience was again somewhere around 1,100 miles in distance from Gig Harbor, Washington to St. George, Utah. The first move was in pursuit of the "American Dream," ownership of our very own home. The second move was in pursuit of *"Every Parent's Dream;" happy teenage children making good choices.*

Janna and I have often discussed with each other, our children, and others that there is about a five-year period of time from about age 14 to 19 where decisions are made that will impact the rest of one's life. Unfortunately, this short period of time comes about the time when teenagers are starting to think that their parents are old fogies who don't understand the things of today and also about the time when parents are thinking their children are getting old enough to make decisions on their own. Think about it. One decision late on a Friday or Saturday night can change the course of your life, for good, or not so good, or very not good. Most of the time though, it is the many smaller decisions made over this period of time that dictate the course our life will follow. Try as we may, as parents, ultimately these life-changing decisions are left up to the inexperience of the young. Our son Kevin said not too long ago. "Why didn't you just (figuratively speaking) punch me in the face a couple of times and make me listen?"

At this pivotal time in our older daughter's life we felt that her decision-making environment wasn't a good one and needed to be changed. As all young teenage girls do, our daughter was doodling on one of her school folders and in so doing jotted down her first name along with several last names of boys in which she was associated. That evening, as she was doing some homework, Janna caught a glimpse of her daughter's name alongside these prospective boyfriends or, as the writing suggested, prospective husbands. Janna, never forgetting a name and a face, and being the Gig Harbor

Little League President for a few years, knew the boy behind each of the names she saw on the school folder. Along with a few other problems Lorraine was having, we were worried. Needless to say, that evening in our room we had a discussion. Our second moving experience begins as we were pondering our options to change our daughter's environment.

It was Christmas time, 2000. Brad had graduated from high school and having completed college credits in high school, was about to begin his last semester of an Associate Degree. Lorraine was a cheerleader in the middle of her junior year of high school. Kevin was wrestling and playing basketball in middle school. Megan was in the fifth grade. Janna had graduated from the University of Washington a few years earlier and was working at the Tacoma Community College, Gig Harbor Branch. I was working at an engineering firm in Tacoma as a designer and project manager. We were comfortable; we were established in the community, but because of strong promptings we knew that a change was coming in the near future. We just didn't know what, when, or how.

There were a couple of employment opportunities back in Southern California, so we decided to go visit the grandparents in Simi Valley for the holidays and follow up with these opportunities. We spent some nice relaxing time with our families which gave us time to think, but after pondering and following up on these job opportunities, I didn't feel strongly one way or the other.

One morning, I got up early and hiked up to one of my favorite childhood spots in the hills to see if I could gain some direction to our problem. As I was hiking up to the top of Mount McCoy in Simi Valley, I pondered heavily on our situation. It reminded me of 11 years earlier when we were faced with a similar dilemma of whether or not to move. Upon reaching the top and taking a brief moment to rest and enjoy the view, I then knelt in prayer. I asked Heavenly Father to show us the way we should go. To show us the way that would be of the most benefit to us, to our children, and to Him. I specifically talked to my Heavenly Father about the different opportunities that had been presented to me and if I should choose one of them. A distinct feeling came over me that yes, moving was the right idea but that no, neither of these current opportunities was the right one. I should keep looking and be open to the Spirit.

We went home from our vacation, got back to work, and a few days later received a phone call with an opportunity that sounded like it just might work. My younger brother Brian was experiencing some growing pains in his construction company with a lot of out of state work and was wondering if I might be interested in coming to the Cedar City, Utah area. Within a few weeks, Janna and I made a trip to Southern Utah. We visited Cedar City, Enterprise and St. George. We drove around neighborhoods, visited high schools and we even went to a basketball game. Janna and I prayed about it, felt good about it and immediately made preparations for our second eleven hundred mile plus journey.

Two months later, we were living on Indian Hills Drive in St. George, Utah. Some people didn't understand why we left Gig Harbor, but our move to St. George had many of the same characteristics as our previous move, including the ease and speed of the decision, the way things worked out smoothly, even the exact location in which we settled, and especially the fact that we absolutely felt that the Lord knows us, cares about us, and wants us to be doing the right thing.

During our first visit to St. George, we felt particularly good about one specific area. Janna and I were attracted to the area of the city where the kids would attend the newest high school out of the three that were in town. While back in Gig Harbor, Janna went through the normal channels to try and locate a rental home in that area. One was located that we thought would fit our needs. I was now working for Brian and was working on a project in the Phoenix, Arizona area. We thought it might be prudent for one of us to visit the potential home before we made a commitment. On the weekend, I drove up from Phoenix and made a second visit to St. George. The home didn't feel quite right to me and through some divine help I was able to locate another choice. It was half of a duplex, which wasn't our first choice, but it felt good, so I filled out the paperwork to begin the rental process.

There is much more to the story. It turned out that although the new choice of our home was in our perceived preferred high school boundaries when we rented the home, it would not be in the desired boundaries the following school year. Thank goodness that prayers are not always answered how you want them to be. We were grateful in the following years, for various reasons, to be part of a different high school. It also turned out that a new little subdivision was just getting started on the other side of the back wall from the duplex in which we moved to. We ended up being able to purchase the building lot directly behind our rental unit and with the kids' help we were able to build the home in which we now live.

We knew that this move was only an opportunity for change. It would be up to our children to desire to take this new circumstance and these new surroundings and make the proper decisions that would set their life course in the proper direction.

The following months were emotional for me as I witnessed the happiness of youth come back into the face of our daughter. Not to say that all of the turmoil of being a teenager had gone away. It hadn't. All of the normal problems were still there, even some extras brought on by the move. The least of which was being yanked out of one high school and starting in a new one near the end of her junior year. But she was handling all of these problems with a new light and happiness, which both she and we enjoyed.

I have often wished to thank those who helped make this change in our lives and helped to save one of our daughters from what could have been a spiritual disaster. Thank you to my previous employer at Sitts and Hill Engineers, whose understanding helped immensely with my own emotional well-being during this period, and to my brother who gave us the opportunity for employment and a change of life here in Southern Utah.

11
Baseball Field Notes

What happens during the game is more important than the game

If you were able to count all of the baseball caps stored throughout our house, you might think that I have been coaching baseball for 50 years. I can't just throw these hats away; they all have memories. It hasn't been 50 years, but if it had been, I would have enjoyed every minute of it. Well, maybe not every minute. The first couple of seasons I had to learn a few things and I wish that I could do those over again. And then there were those couple of hours after a loss in which I probably wasn't much good for anything and had to take a nap. Come to think of it, win or lose, I took a nap after every game. I coached officially for about eight years, and then after moving to St. George helped as an assistant for another season. During those eight or so years while coaching a team, I was usually also assisting on one or more of the other kids' teams. I also had fun umpiring many baseball games and I even had the opportunity to help coach a fourth and fifth grade football team.

Probably the most important thing I learned from coaching is this: The game is for the kids. Not you as the coach, not the parents, just the kids. So if your focus as a coach is what is going to be the most benefit to the greatest number, if not all the kids, then you will have a good start on correctly doing the coaching/teaching/helping job you signed up for. What I tried to do to help me in this area was to follow my own philosophy that I used in my profession as a General Contractor. When a question came up on how to handle a particular problem, I would think to myself, "How would I do it, or fix this, if this was my own home?" This relates to coaching, "How would you do this if this was your own child playing?" In other words, treat each player as if they were your own child.

Early on I heard a quote, "A child would rather play and lose, than not play at all." I found this statement to be very true. To add to that, I also learned that parents would rather see their child play and lose than not have their child play at all.

Gig Harbor wasn't a small town, but it was small enough that you would occasionally see team members and parents while shopping or enjoying pizza at the local hangout or at some other function. I learned that things that happened during the game (such as the amount of playing time and having fun) had much more lasting consequences than whether we posted a win or not. It was much more enjoyable to meet a mom in the grocery store if her child was having a good experience rather than a not so good one, for whatever reason.

I also learned from my own kids that win or lose, when the game is over, it is over, and they are on to next fun thing. When I was feeling down after a loss and wanting to go take a nap, they would come running up and say something like, "Can I go over to Seth's house and ride bikes?"

I would think to myself, "No, you have to come home and be sad for a while. Then you can go ride bikes." But of course I was glad for them. The game was over and they were on to the next thing. Losing wasn't that big of a deal. The only thing they remembered when it came to playing was whether or not they were having fun. Now, if you can build confidence and character in your players, keep the parents happy, and if the kids are having fun and winning all at the same time, then possibly you're on the right track. Don't get me wrong, we did everything we could to try to win, winning is fun, just don't sacrifice a child to do it.

I recall one particularly memorable moment for me. It was early on in our season. I cannot remember the particulars of this specific game, just after it was over. The game ended, and one of the boys who was new to our team this year was still sitting on the bench after most of the kids had left the dug-out. I noticed that he had a funny look on his face. I asked him how he was doing and if he was okay.

He turned his head, looked at me and asked, "What is going on? Where did everybody go?"

I said, "What do you mean. The game is over."

He said, "It can't be over."

I asked, "Why not?"

His reply was, "Well, I have been playing first base the whole time." Now I was puzzled. With a tear in his eye he continued, "I have never played the whole game before."

I put my hand on his shoulder and said something like, "Well, now you have and you did a great job." It was clearly a meaningful moment for him and a real teaching moment for me. Interestingly, the following season at our preseason team meeting, some of the returning players and parents referred to me as Coach Dan. His parents referred to me as Reverend Dan.

We moved to St. George in the spring of 2000, just prior to Little League tryouts. Kevin was almost 14 and was now in what Little League called the Senior League. The area in which we lived was in the Snow Canyon Little League district, because then we were also in the Snow Canyon High School boundaries. The following year the boundaries would be changed and we would be in the Dixie High School boundaries.

Tryouts are designed so that as all the boys go through a little routine, the team managers and coaches can see all of the players and their abilities. Then a draft is held and the boys are drafted/chosen to a team. This is Little League's designed way of forming fairly balanced teams. Interestingly, it turns out that all of the new kids that had moved in over the past year or were new to playing baseball ended up on the same team. The team manager was also new to the area. Since I had been previously involved in the try-out process for many years, this seemed a little bit fishy. But we were here to play so we didn't get too excited about it.

Because I was working out of town at the time, I didn't think I was going to be able to be of much assistance. Somehow my schedule worked out and I was able to help at most practices and attend most of the games. We had a great season, and I am sure much to the dismay of the other long-time coaches, this new team of boys won the league. As is the tradition in most leagues, the winning coach or manager gets the privilege of managing the All-star team with the other team managers as assistants. Kevin, along with a few other boys from his team, was chosen to participate on this team. One of the other new boys to the area, TJ, also lived in the area which would be part of the Dixie High boundaries the following year. Kevin and TJ had been an important part of the success of the team during the regular season. Kevin had played shortstop, both pitched, and both had done well at the plate. TJ was the best batter on the team, batting in the "4 spot", the "clean-up batter".

 The newly formed All-star team was doing well and had won their first two games. Oddly, in the third game, a game that if won would put the team into the finals, Kevin and TJ were mostly sitting on the bench. It was a little unusual, but to be fair, rotations do need to be made. Unfortunately, because of some key errors at key positions, this game was lost. The team still had a chance to go to the finals and on to the state play-offs, if they could win the rest of their games. Kevin and TJ still mostly sat on the bench in the following game. That game too was lost, and the season was over.

 At some point after the season the coach apologized and divulged the rest of the story. During the second game the president of Snow Canyon Little League asked our coach why he was playing those two boys. Our coach replied, "What two boys?"

 The league president said, "The two boys who will be playing for Dixie High School next year."

Coach said, "Because they are my best players." After some discussion the coach said he became intimidated and was told not to play the two Dixie boys. This president's behavior was probably the most blatant display of grown-ups losing sight of why kids play baseball that I have ever seen. Remember the game is for the players, not for the parents or some perceived rivalry that may take place in the future.

The second most important thing I learned from coaching is always build up the player; never tear them down. I learned that you will always get more from a player when you give praise and show confidence in them. You will not only get more from them, you will also improve your players' abilities both on and off the field or court. That's your job. The whole idea behind school/youth sports should be improving the young person's abilities both on and off the field. It was very surprising to me to learn, as my children moved up from Little League to high school sports, that coaches in these upper levels do not know or understand this simple principle. As I think back over the number of coaches that I have known, only one stands out as fully understanding this principle. That is a sad percentage. I can think of a few others that were progressing towards this understanding, but I can also think of a lot of others who have been coaching for a long time and were not getting any closer to understanding what coaching at these age groups is all about.

For example, when your pitcher is struggling and you approach the pitcher's mound, do you yank him at the first mistake? Do you yell, "One more bad pitch and you're out," or do you help him relax and tell him he is a good pitcher and that he can do this? On one occasion during a particularly close game back in Gig Harbor, Kevin was brought in to pitch. After struggling to get us out of the inning and upon returning to the dugout he said to me that he didn't feel very good and somebody else should pitch. Following the example of the only good coach I knew, I said, "Kevin you're a good pitcher. You are it. You are my third pitcher of the game. We don't have anybody else who can pitch tonight. Just relax and do your best." Well, with a good offensive half of the inning and a few more positive trips to the mound in the next inning, we pulled off a win.

Contrast that with this story. Kevin had been pitching since age nine. He had always been a good pitcher that you could count on, not an overpowering pitcher but a smart pitcher. While he was in the 10th grade and playing in the high school organization those who were pitchers and wanted to pitch that season were asked to spend time with the team's pitching coach. While Kevin was taking his pitching instruction, he was told that he would never make a good pitcher. According to this particular coach, his throwing technique was not correct. This so-called pitching coach was right; Kevin never did make a good pitcher. Kevin never tried to pitch again. How strange and tragic, since for the previous six or seven years he had done quite well and had been a starting pitcher on at least six All-star teams. Although he continued to play at various positions for the next two-and-a-half years, I watched

Kevin's desire to work hard at baseball and his true sense of fun slowly diminish.

High school basketball was the same way. We watched for three years as different, very talented Varsity team players slowly lost their confidence and desire to play because they spent more and more time being coached by a Varsity coach who could not compliment, only punish. We watched for three years as our Varsity teams lost all close and tense games in the fourth quarter as their excitement, enthusiasm and confidence was overwhelmed by the negative techniques of the coach.

To conclude, number one, remember: the game is for the players. *What happens during the game is more important than the game.* Number two: Be positive and uplifting. Build the players ability and confidence for life; build men and women. If you are going to coach, (or be a dad), it is a lot more important to be able to relate to the age group you are coaching than it is to have been a good player at one time in the past.

12
Scouting Notes

To be a builder of boys you must provide adventure

It was a dark and stormy night in Gig Harbor, Washington. Well, most of the time it was dark and stormy, or at least gray and drizzly. We were all meeting at the church parking lot on a Friday evening in preparation for our monthly overnight campout. Parents dropped off the younger boys, teenagers gathered stuff from the back of their beater cars, and a few Dads hustled in after trying to pack their back-packs after work. Permission slips were gathered and eventually we would be ready to brave the Northwest weather and head into the wilderness. Good times. As the Scoutmaster, one thing I didn't do as we gathered was to perform the customary backpack check. I had learned as a young scout that if a boy learned the hard way how to pack a pack, then that would be the last time his pack was outfitted improperly.

As a young boy, I had the privilege of attending many a scout hike with my Dad's troop of 14 to 15 year old boys, including a 50-mile hike at age 10. In the typical training for that hike, (and since I only weighed about 70 pounds) I had learned how to pack light but sufficiently.

At age 13 my friend David and I were the senior leaders in a troop that had just received a new Scoutmaster. Excited about his new calling, this new

Scoutmaster was up for the challenge for his and his son's first hike. David and I planned a hike that we had done previously. It was about a three-mile hike down to a river that had a beautiful campsite in the trees along the river's edge. We figured that the hike in would be an easy down-hill hike for the new scouts.

We arrived late in the afternoon, and although it was in the dark, the trek down was relatively easy and all was well when we reached the camp. As we set up camp and began to prepare our meals, I was amazed to see what transpired as our new scout and his Scoutmaster dad began to cook dinner. First out of the backpacks came a couple of steaks that looked more like roasts. Then, even much more to my amazement, Our Scoutmaster pulled out a 10 inch cast iron frying pan, full bottle of oil, table size salt and pepper shakers and plates and silverware. Being a little embarrassed, the Scoutmaster explained that his wife had packed their packs for them. I don't remember what David's and my meal consisted of, but I do remember as we were washing up our little mess kits, their steaks had just barely begun to brown.

The next morning was about the same; David and I were off to explore the wilds while they were still in the midst of breakfast preparations. After a day of having fun playing around the river, it became time for the troop to pack up and head back up the trail to the cars. David was asked to lead out to set the pace and to keep all scouts between him and myself, who would bring up the rear. The new Scoutmaster and his son headed out with David and the rest of the boys followed.

Shortly thereafter I came upon the Scoutmaster and his son on the side of the trail. I recall that the Scoutmaster had removed the cast iron frying pan from his back-pack and was placing it into his son's pack. Well, as you can guess, that didn't work out, and to avoid spending that night on the trail, I was asked to trade packs with the young scout. David, the scouts, the new additions to the troop and me, (carrying a cast iron frying pan) finally made it to the top of the hill. Needless to say, on the next trip some lightweight equipment had been purchased, backpacks were packed by the individuals who would be carrying them and all future hikes were much more enjoyable.

As a Scoutmaster in Gig Harbor, I didn't perform a pack check, but I always carried an extra sweatshirt, socks, and a trash bag (for use as a raincoat) in case it was needed by an unprepared boy. Proper equipment and packing techniques were discussed at length in our weekly meetings and a backpack check list was provided for both boy and mom. Although to this date I have never again seen a 10 inch cast iron skillet being pulled from a backpack, it has been fun over the years to watch the many young men change from young scouts to seasoned backpackers. From the above experience and many others, I determined that backpacking, not just camping, needed to be an essential part of the scouting experience. How else can a boy learn so quickly to be prepared, to depend on his own planning and to have that planning be evident in the contents of his backpack? In backpacking, for the few days you're out on the trail, everything you own and depend on for safety and comfort is on your back.

I remember watching one young scout, on an early spring hike, tromp through the snow and puddles, most of which he could have gone around or stepped over. As you would expect, he got to camp with wet, freezing feet. I watched as he lay in his sleeping bag trying to warm his feet while holding a lighter under his boots to dry them. Knowing that the young scout would not be able to participate in the rest of the activities with wet boots, one of the other leaders on the trip felt sorry for him and eventually built a nice cozy fire to warm his feet and to dry his boots.

I watched one dad, who was generously taking the time to go camping with his son, run to the hardware store to buy a tent as we were fueling the vehicles and leaving town. Needless to say the hardware store tent did not hold up to the Northwest weather and it was a long wet, but, memorable experience for them.

Before we undertook a long hike or adventure, it was required that the scouts who would participate in the adventure attend the many training activities and hikes we scheduled. These prepared scouts would always confidently outperform the adults who came along on those adventures without participating in the training.

I learned a wonderful lesson from my older son as we undertook one particularly hard outing. This outing was so hard that the troop was not invited until we, as a few adults, and my son Brad, age 13, experienced it first. We adults were extending our own training. Living in the Northwest we had some wonderful places to go and we were enjoying learning about and trying mountain climbing. A few of us had previously climbed (or maybe I should say crawled) Mt. Rainier and were wondering if some of the less dangerous peaks would be appropriate for the scouts.

One such peak was Mt. Adams. According to the guide book and maps, the trail- head for the climb of Mt. Adams was about a four-hour drive away. The climb would take about 8 hours to reach the top at approximately 12,276 feet. Because we were unable to leave the afternoon before, we left home at 1:00 am so as to be on the trail as close to 5:00 am as possible. It was a long, grueling, bumpy road to the trailhead; at least it seemed like it to the passengers trying to get some much needed sleep. As was expected, it was an even longer grueling hike and climb to the top. We saw other hikers on the trail, some had camped at the trailhead and others had camped about halfway up on the mountain. Few of these summit hopefuls actually made it to the top. About 14 hours after departing from Gig Harbor we finally crested the summit. We rested and enjoyed the view for a short time, and then with weak jello-y legs we began the trek back down 7,000 feet to the vehicle.

At about 8:00 PM that evening, still about a mile from the truck, I was having a hard time putting one foot in front of the other and continuing in a forward motion. Fearing that Brad at least felt the same way I did, if not worse, for he had suffered from some altitude sickness earlier in the day, I was trying to say some positive things and asked him how he was doing.

Sounding vaguely like the scholars of old who came up with the phrase: "This too shall pass," Brad said something like, "Yeah, I am pretty tired, but I know soon we will be at the truck and then I will be able to sit down for a long time and we will stop and get lots of food to eat." He was right. We did stop and eat lots of good food and approximately 24 hours after we had left, we arrived back at home.

The next big climb, about a year later on Mt. Baker, Brad lead the way and left me in the dust or I should say snow. I have never worried about his physical or emotional abilities since.

We had many wonderful outings over several years of scouting. The boys did get the opportunity to do some mountain climbing. As a troop we climbed Mt. Olympus, Mt. Adams and some had the opportunity to climb Mt. Baker. With a few of the stronger boys, we even attempted Mt. Rainier, but because of severe weather at about 13,000 feet, we felt it wise to turn back. In addition to mountain climbing and many other outings, twice we accomplished the 50-mile-long Press Expedition Trail in the Olympic National Park. We hiked along the coastline in the northernmost corner of Washington State and we floated 100 miles down the Grande Ronde River in Oregon. What a lot of great memories.

Note to all Scoutmasters' Wives: Thank you for your support. When we were planning a week of high adventure in the northwest, the first week in August was our best shot for good weather. Consequently our scout calendar usually had this week set aside for this activity.

Janna was a great sport; our anniversary is August 7th and we typically had to celebrate it a week late.

I had an experience at Scout Camp that sums up my feelings and counsel relating to Scouting. One year, as I sat in on a merit badge workshop with some of the younger boys in our troop, this took place. Scout Camp is mostly staffed with older, more advanced and experienced scouts who are about age 17 and are mostly all Eagle Scouts. As I sat there and the boys worked on the merit badge, the Eagle Scout running the workshop came over and asked me about the hat I was wearing. I explained that when our troop went on a High Adventure outing each year, we had hats made up for those who went. They could wear the hat on the outing and keep it afterwards for a memento. I don't remember if this particular hat was for our Mt. Olympus climb or for our Grand Ronde River trip. After showing the young man the hat, I could still see some questions on his face, so I explained the particulars of the outing. When I finished telling my story he said, "Wow, I wish I could go on something like that."

I asked, "What do you mean? What kind of High Adventure has your troop done?" He explained that car camping, camporees and week long Scout Camp was all that their troop had done.

Sadly, I am afraid that this young man's story is all too common in Scouting. My philosophy is that, *To be a builder of boys, you must provide adventure.* Learning the Scout Motto, "Be Prepared," will naturally occur and even spiritual experiences will be had as boys learn what can be accomplished in a tough situation with a little hard work.

As I was finishing this chapter, my son Kevin wrote from his mission in Argentina. He recalled hiking Mount Adams with our troop. This submission came unsolicited from him. He was twelve at the time of our hike. I will quote his words from the letter,

"I remembered something the other day, Dad, that was cool. We were fasting and I thought I was going to die. It reminded me of when we were climbing Mount Adams, and I didn't really eat breakfast the morning of climbing to the summit, and I started crying because I was so out of energy and about to die. I thought to myself, ha ha, good times. I think they were Skittles that saved my life." Because Kevin had survived this tough time on our climb of Mt. Adams and others with fond memories, he can now handle other hard situations with more confidence.

My counsel to dads is to be involved with your sons in Scouting. You will have experiences that will last a life time. My counsel to Scoutmasters is to provide adventure and get the parents involved. As a new Scoutmaster I had two thoughts that I had hoped would and did help me in this area. First, I set a goal to be a backpacking troop and not a car camping troop, thus providing a greater opportunity for real adventure. Secondly, I decided to carry a video camera on all of our outings. I recorded the young men having fun and working hard in the beautiful Northwest out-of-doors.

The first few outings were attended by a relatively small group of boys and, as usual in Scouting, very few if any dads. Our troop was sponsored by the LDS Church, so I decided to show a short 5 minute video clip of our outings to all of the young and older men the following Sunday morning after our trips. These video showings accomplished two wonderful things. First, older young men, who had once figured that Scouting was too childish for them, decided that our trips looked fun and decided to participate. Secondly, dads also decided that our outings looked fun and figured out that they could be enjoying some great experiences with their sons. Our troop participation began to grow and it was not unusual to have quite a few 16 and 17 year old Scouts and a large number of dads on all of our outings.

I learned another very important Scouting fact from this experience. If a boy's parents are what I labeled "scouting inactive," meaning the dad did not take the opportunity to at least attend outings and or the mom was not involved with the Scout Committee, then it was very difficult, almost impossible for the young man to achieve the worldwide recognized Scouting rank of Eagle Scout.

As a side note; the video footage I had collected over the years came in very handy at Eagle Award Courts of Honor. I would go back through the videos and put together a short collection of clips of the young man from his first outing as a young scout, to the date of his Court of Honor. We would show the short adventure film at the Court of Honor and then present it to him and his mom.

13
The Two A's

Adventure & Attention

A few years ago Janna asked me this question, "After being a Scoutmaster for many years, what is the most important thing you learned about boys?"

I replied, "That's easy, all boys need adventure."

She then asked, "What do you think girls need?"

I replied "Aaaaaaa, hmmmm, I guess I am not sure what girls need."

Thinking on her years of experience with young women, she replied; "If adventure is the most important motivator for boys, then for girls it is attention. Girls need attention." We further discussed the topic and concluded that both answers were absolutely correct. Boys need *adventure* and girls need *attention*. If either of them doesn't get adventure or attention at home, they will seek it from other places and we can all imagine plenty of worldly sources where one could go for both of them. A lot of moms give their girls attention, but sometimes, especially when girls get a little older, attention from mom is perceived as nagging. So what girls really need is attention from dad.

On occasion, someone in our family will get out one of the family picture albums to look through. Those at home will usually gather around to reminisce on fond memories. For years when this happened, the look back at memory lane would always be interrupted by our youngest, Megan, who would say something like, "There aren't very many pictures of me. You guys don't love me." We would reassure her that we did love her just as much as the other children. Although Janna and I always felt a little guilty that our exuberance for taking pictures of the kids had worn off by child number four.

Recently, I have been going through all of our old videos and transferring them to the computer hard drive. In doing so I discovered the cause for the lack of photos of Megan in the family album. About the time she was born (1990) we invested in a video camera and for the next several years, most photo opportunities were captured on video instead of the old fashioned still shot camera.

It was fun to discover that we have plenty of footage of Megan. We can now prove that we did indeed love her just as much as everyone else. Now she gets tired of me calling her to the computer to watch herself crawling around the living room floor, or giggling, or starting to walk, or jumping on the trampoline, or many other cute baby and toddler activities. In fact, now that she is the only child left at home, whether she likes it or not, she is getting all of the attention that might have been lacking while growing up as the youngest child. She is even making up for any lost lap time. With only three of us at home, there is plenty of sitting space on the living room furniture. But as Janna or I sit down to relax a moment, Megan will wander over and decide it is time to wrestle, or sit on one of our laps and watch TV. She is 17 ½ and a senior in high school but we enjoy it.

Sometimes as men it might seem difficult to relate to and give attention to our young and/or teenage daughters. I have found that girls will enjoy anything that their dad enjoys, if they are invited to participate. They will play on the Little League baseball team, they will go hiking and camping, they will go on an adventurous white water river rafting trip, they will help you build a house or two, and they really enjoy driving the Jeep on a rough trail. If coaxed properly with a new pair of coveralls to wear, they may even help you work on cars in the garage. They can beat you in badminton and they will beat you at Guitar Hero. Along with tea parties, swinging on a swing, or just laying in the hammock together, there are plenty of activities to enjoy with our girls.

14
The Joys Of Parenthood
(A compilation of short stories)

What The......

It was a dark and stormy night. That's not really true but this story will still give you a good scare. From 1986 thru 1989 we lived in Solvang, California. Most of our time in Solvang we lived in a rental house that was near the road but located in the middle of about a 40 acre parcel that was used to grow tomatoes. In about 1988 Brad was 6 years old, Lorraine was 4 and Kevin was 1 year old.

This jolt to our hearts took place on a typical weekday evening. We had dinner, cleaned up a little, watched a little TV, gave the kids their baths, and then got them into their jammies. As usual, the older two did not want to go to bed at this time, but it was a school night for Brad and schedules needed to be kept. Prayers were said and the kids tucked in. The lights were turned off and the door left slightly ajar.

Our little rental home in the middle of the tomato patch was a small two-bedroom home and all three kids slept in the same room. It seems as though that night there were the typical minor sounds and the traditional, "I need a drink of water" but eventually, all was quiet and we settled down to relax and watch a little TV.

Sometime later, as we began to prepare for bed ourselves, we went in to check on the kids and to perform the final blanket adjustments, etc... As we opened the door to go in, our stomachs jumped, and one of us said rather loudly, "What the ....", we could see that the bunk beds were empty. A quick glance around the rest of the room showed that Kevin was still asleep in his crib, but the other two were not visible. Our hearts began to race as we looked under the beds and then in our bedroom to see if they had slipped into our bed. The quick search came up empty. Trying hard to resist panic, we checked in corners and closets. We looked in the only other room in the house, the laundry room. We rechecked under beds. No sign of them anywhere.

      Upon reentering the master bedroom we noticed the curtain move slightly and we went over to find that the window was open and the screen was not in place. We ran outside and looked around the house and the small fenced yard. Still, no sign. Our small home had a cedar slat fence around it to give some privacy from the fairly busy road out front and the farming activities on the other three sides. The one car garage and gravel driveway were outside the front gate and fence. Near panic now, we exited the gate to look along the road. No sign of them out front either. Now in full panic mode, our next option was to run back in the house and call the police. Wait. As we looked at our car parked in the driveway, we wondered why the two front seats of our little Hyundai were in the reclined position. We looked in the window and saw our two naughty little children asleep in the car.

Hitting the Brakes

Next is a story I hesitate to tell, for fear that the reader may think we are the rottenest parents ever. It was a Saturday afternoon and Kevin was having his birthday. He was turning 4 years old. The birthday plans were to go as a family to the movies and see "Teenage Mutant Ninja Turtles."

Kevin's two favorite toys at this time were a plywood sword I had made him from scraps while building our house and another homemade toy I had fashioned for a Halloween costume accessory, nunchuks. He loved his little weapons and the Ninja Turtles and I can't remember if it was before or after this event that Kevin used his wooden sword to fight the neighbor's newly planted pink dogwood tree. The little sapling had lost the fight and we had to replace it for the old grumpy neighbor.

Anyway, as we headed to the movies in our family van, Brad and Lorraine began to fight about something, I have no idea what. After our repeated attempts to settle things, I finally said something like, "If you can't settle down and get along, I am going to pull over and you will have to walk home and miss the movie." They must have been on a roll, because that threat didn't faze them and I had no choice but to pull over and kick them out. As I hit the brakes and pulled the van over in front of Finholm's Market, they became quiet. I don't think any of us knew what was going to happen next. Finholm's Market is about three miles along a rural route from our home. The two were asked to get out of the van, which they did, and told to walk straight home. Their faces and ours were sad as Janna and I, Kevin and Megan drove away. Of course, Janna and I could not relax during the movie and we certainly didn't wait for the credits to roll as we rushed home.

When we arrived home, Brad and Lorraine were sitting on the couch watching TV, smiling and happy. It was as though two best friends had gone on an adventure. We asked them how their journey was. They related that after walking about halfway and just prior to having to walk up Drummond (a big, long, uphill road), that Lorraine's previous kindergarten teacher, who lived in our neighborhood, had come by and asked them if they needed a ride. They told her they did and were driven the rest of the way home. We figured that since Brad was only about eight-and-a-half and Lorraine was about six-and- a-half that we would hear from the school teacher later, but we never did.

Over the years I can remember just needing to tap the brakes and head for the side of the road in order to get things calmed down and quiet for a good long time. Sometimes just for fun I would hit the brakes and head for the side of the road, just to see the panic in their faces. Then we would all laugh.

Superman

One Saturday evening Janna and I planned a date night, the basic dinner and a movie with some friends. Our 14 year old nephew was staying with us for a few days so we thought that he could be the sitter for the evening. Brad, our oldest, was about eleven. We made the usual arrangements necessary for younger kids: a Kraft macaroni and cheese with hotdogs dinner, baths, pajamas, etc. We explained the usual guidelines to our nephew, various bed times and where we would be in case of an emergency, etc. All seemed to be normal as we said our goodbyes and left for the evening.

We enjoyed the relaxing time chitchatting over a nice meal. Soon it was time for us to head to the theater. Standing outside the Gig Harbor Cinemas, we were disappointed to find that from the two selections available, neither movie was worth seeing. Sometimes we would drive across the bridge to Tacoma to find another theater, but that didn't sound good either, so we decided to call it an early evening and headed for home.

We turned into the neighborhood and came around the corner and, as is typical when returning home, took a quick survey of the house. Good, no smoke. We pulled into the driveway and casually walked to the front door. We opened the door just in time to see Brad's body flash by. It couldn't be true, but thinking back over the many years, and seeing it in slow motion, it seems as though it was in a Superman pose, only in a downward projection. Luckily, at the same instant, we could also see the giant pile of cushions and pillows piled up at the intended landing point.

Our home had a two story great room. At the top of the stairs, the landing overlooked the room below. Somebody, during the evening, had the great idea of gathering all of the couch cushions and bed pillows they could find and building a makeshift foam pit so that various stunt jumps could be performed. Apparently all the kids tried the jump.

Brad's landing was successful and when the shock subsided and we could move our frozen bodies, we continued through the door. I mentioned intended landing point because on second look, we could see Lorraine sitting awkwardly on the couch (with no cushions on it) with tears in her eyes. Yes, that's right, after much coaxing from her baby sitter and her older brother she did exactly what your mom has always told you not to do, jump off something just because somebody told you to. In this case it wasn't a bridge; it was the railing on the upper stair landing. Lorraine, jumping cautiously, didn't quite jump far enough and landed Indian style on one lone pillow from about 12 feet up. Luckily, no permanent damage occurred.

Although cousin Sterling was a kind and loving boy, he did have a mischievous side and we used more caution in choosing sitters from then on.

Redneck Yacht Club

When we were thinking about buying our lot on Crescent Lake Drive, we knew there was a cool little lake just at the bottom of the street. Crescent Lake was a small lake that we thought would be a lot of fun and perfect for our little family. The only problem with the lake was that there were houses mostly all around it, and the areas that didn't have houses were totally over grown, so it was very hard, almost impossible, to get to the lake. Before we bought the property, we saw on a plat map that there was an undeveloped piece of land at the end of our cul-de-sac, which was designated as a city park. This undeveloped parcel was adjacent to the south end of the lake and backed up to 6000 acres of forest which also adjoined the lot that we were about to buy. We figured that this piece of public property would be our own private entrance to the lake. As we were purchasing the property, we were already formulating a plan to get to and use the lake and we also knew that trails in the adjoining woods would be lots of fun too.

While building our house the fall and winter of 1994/1995, we used many of the trees which needed to be cut down in order to make room to build our house, to build the porches and provide the siding. I milled the lumber with a contraption that attached to my chain saw. As a result of cutting flat lumber from a round log, we had a lot of scraps of wood left over that were flat on one side and round on the other.

From the beginning we had planned on making a secret trail to the lake. We scouted around and eventually we made a trail down to the water's edge. Part of the trail was overgrown and you had to duck down a little to avoid tree branches, and part of it was soft and mushy. We tried to make it usable enough for us but camouflaged for everyone else.

After we got settled in the house, when the summer began and the weather got warmer, we decided that a trail to the water's edge wasn't quite enough. After the boys had found a big four-foot piece of Styrofoam floating on the lake and brought it home, we came up with a plan to build our own floating dock. I figured that with some scrap logs and some of the planks that were flat on one side we should be able to build a nice little raft-like dock. Our plan was to build the float and anchor it out from the shore a little ways, so that we would have something to swim to and play on down at the lake at the end of our trail.

We built the framework at the house with 4 logs making a square and notched them so they would sit on each other tight. We then found the best log edge planks for the deck, and cut them to the right length. A couple of 2x4s nailed around the edges would provide the finishing touches to our redneck sun-and-fun floating deck.

We figured out that we would never be able to make this floating deck and then carry it down our little trail to the lake, it would be too heavy. So we loaded all of the pieces of the deck into the back of the truck and drove around to the other side of the lake to the public boat ramp, which was just a gravel road that dead ended into the water. We unloaded everything, set the pieces together at the water's edge, nailed all the parts to one another and built our little float right there on the ramp.

So that our hard work would not get waterlogged and eventually sink, I bought a new piece of Styrofoam to match the other one the boys found and we attached them underneath. We slid the float in the water; the boys got on, put their homemade paddles in the water and started paddling across the lake to the small opening where our secret trail exited the woods. Meanwhile, I drove back around the lake, and walked down the trail to meet them there. The craft wasn't designed for smooth sailing and their paddles were just scrap pieces of wood, so I had to wait a little while for them to arrive. Then we took our homemade anchor, which was a five gallon bucket filled with concrete and a rebar loop at the top, and secured our new float out past the cat tails and the lily pads.

All that summer and many more to follow, we would walk down to the end of our street, down through the trees, the ferns and the salal bushes, on our way to the lake where we would step into the tea-stained water, with the peat moss mud grabbing our ankles, wade out a little ways and swim out to our float. We even had to cut a trail through the lily pads for a swimming path.

We spent a lot of time playing king of the dock, trying to flip the float over and coming up with all kinds of funny dives and jumps off of it. The kids loved to swim up underneath it and breathe in the little pocket of air between the pieces of styrofoam.

Megan learned how to swim off of that float and we never worried about her at all. Except for one time, when she wanted to show us her favorite jump off the dock known as "the pencil." Upon returning to the surface with a somewhat worried look on her face, she frantically stated that she had gone too deep and that her pointed feet had almost got stuck in the mud.

15
Chef Dad

If you are having a BBQ, you can cook and play at the same time

All families need to have some traditions to look back on and recall as they talk about the past. These traditions can be formal such as a Christmas Eve program or they can be informal and irregular such as dad cooking his "Special Recipe."

When we first moved into our Crescent Lake House the basement was the only area that was livable. The rest of the house was still under construction. Our basement kitchen consisted of a few open cabinets, the refrigerator, a microwave oven and a propane camp stove. The kitchen sink was in the bathroom. Although it was a large two basin sink, officially we did not have a kitchen sink. We also did not have an oven. Not having an oven meant that for about a year we had to do without any baked items such as chocolate chip cookies etc. We did learn how to cook brownies in the microwave and to this day brownies remain a family staple.

While working on a kitchen remodeling project in town, I was able to bring home a 35-year-old double oven wall unit. I brought it home complete with the 35-year-old cabinet which housed it and on one Saturday afternoon, I temporarily installed it in what would later become our official kitchen upstairs. To celebrate the addition of the new cooking appliance into our lives, that

Sunday morning I found an old favorite family recipe from when I was young, German Pancakes, and cooked up a large batch. Thus began the family tradition of "Sunday Morning German Pancakes cooked by Dad." I think it was only about six months later when our 75-year-old antique stove and oven unit was installed in our almost finished kitchen and the tradition continued.

My suggestion would be that dads should have at least a handful of easy, delicious recipes that do not come from a can, and that can be whipped up when needed, or just for fun, or for a fun family tradition. To get you started, the following are some simple family fun recipes that any dad can do. Experiment, have fun, and enjoy the family time.

German Pancakes

Preheat oven to 400 degrees
Place clear glass dish in oven.
(Approx. 8"x11" or 9" round)
3 eggs
½ cup flour, stirred and measured
½ cup milk
¼ teaspoon salt
2 tablespoons butter or margarine

Mix eggs, flour, milk and salt in bowl. Beat until smooth, about 3 minutes. Remove dish from oven, be careful, it is really hot, and add butter, rotate dish until butter is melted. Add batter immediately and bake on lowest oven shelf for 18 to 20 minutes or until golden brown. Serve with powdered sugar, jam or syrup.

Note: Figure about 1 ½ eggs per person. The above recipe can easily be doubled, tripled, or quadrupled for the number of people being served. Tripled recipe works well in either a 9"x13" or a 10"x15" dish.

While cooking, turn on the oven light and watch it grow. German Pancakes work well on Sunday mornings. All of our family likes to be present when it comes out of the oven to see it at its best and eat it while it is hot. What better way to start off Sunday than with everybody gathered around for a fun and interesting breakfast.

Fry Bread

1 cup milk
2 cups flour
1 Tbsp baking powder
1 tsp salt

Mix all ingredients, let stand for 5 – 10 minutes. If dough is too sticky add a few pinches of flour. Roll out a golf ball size chunk at a time. Fry in hot oil. Top with jam.
Feeds about 4

Variations: Top with pizza toppings or taco fixings.

It is always fun to make different shapes and to have family members guess what the fried bread is supposed to resemble.

Macaroni and Cheese

1 ½ cups macaroni	3 tbsp flour
2 quarts boiling water	4 tbsp margarine
1 tsp salt	½ tsp salt
2 cups milk	1 cup grated cheddar cheese

Add 1 tsp. salt to water and bring to a boil. Add macaroni to boiling water, bring back to a boil and reduce heat.

To make the white sauce; melt the butter in a sauce pan, add flour slowly and whisk until there are no lumps, add milk one cup at a time, let thicken between cups of milk. Add ½ tsp. salt to sauce and stir until slightly thick. Add cheese and stir until melted.

Cook the macaroni until tender. Drain. Mix macaroni and cheese sauce in a buttered baking dish. Sprinkle top with grated cheese. Bake until sauce bubbles, about 20 minutes at 400 F. Can be served without baking if you like it saucier.

Variations: Add hot dog, Italian or Polish sausage pieces to the noodles a few minutes before they are done.

Egg in Toast
(An easy favorite)
eggs
butter
bread
salt and pepper

Melt a pat of butter in frying pan. Cut a hole in the middle of a slice of bread, about 1-3/4 inches in diameter. Place bread in heated pan; crack an egg into the hole in the bread, lightly salt egg. Cook until toasted, flip toast and egg and cook until egg is to your liking.

Note: Works well with all breads, exceptional with Sourdough or Italian artisan bread.

Potato Bar

Potatoes
Butter
Sour cream or ranch dressing
Grated cheddar cheese
Chopped cooked bacon or bacon bits
Beanless chili (optional)
Onions (optional)

Clean potatoes without peeling. Microwave on high until fork inserts easily. Slice open potato and pile on the toppings to your liking.

Chili Dogs and Chili Burgers

Hot dogs or burgers
Buns
Beanless chili
Grated cheddar cheese
Onions (optional)
Sliced tomatoes (optional)

Cook dogs or burgers and heat up the chili. Place meat in bun. Spoon on chili and add cheese. For an adult favorite gourmet burger, BBQ the meat and add a fresh slice of tomato on the chili burger.

Note: The secret to great BBQ hamburgers is lower heat and fresh meat.

Caramel Pop Corn

2 cups brown sugar, packed
½ cup (1 stick) butter or margarine
½ cup light corn syrup
5 quarts popped corn (separate un-popped kernels)

Combine sugar, butter and corn syrup in heavy saucepan. Cook and stir over medium heat until sugar dissolves and mixture boils. Simmer for 5 minutes. Remove from heat. Pour over popped corn, stirring until all corn is coated. Turn out onto clean cool cookie sheet or wax paper and spread out. When thoroughly cooled, break into pieces.

Note: You can experiment with the cooking time. Example, simmering for 4 minutes will result in chewier Caramel Corn. Butter flavored microwave popcorn works well and adds an extra buttery flavor.

Caramel Pop Corn has been a family favorite ever since our oldest was little. It is also one of our family's favorite goodies to make at Christmas time. In fact, on several occasions we split up a fresh batch into two or three decoratively packaged gifts to deliver while caroling. Back when we could still talk Brad into doing things he didn't want to do, we would have him bring his saxophone and accompany us as we sang "We Wish You Merry Christmas" to some bewildered friends.

My suggestion to all dads is: Have as many BBQs in the backyard as possible. Keep it simple so you can have fun. Play a game of catch, or pickle, or build a family pyramid while you are watching the cooking. *If you are having a BBQ, you can cook and play at the same time.* Cook your special recipes whenever possible, it can be a big help around the house and you might even start a family tradition of your own.

16
Beyond 50 Years

We don't have to be great scholars of doctrine but we do need to be men of action

"Children are more influenced by sermons you act than by sermons you preach" David O. McKay, 1955

I enjoy the above quote, because one of the areas in which I greatly lack is my speaking skills. I can have something very clear in my mind, and then as I try to express it, it doesn't seem to come out as clearly. Sometimes, when we were gathered around the dinner table, I would tell the family that I had a topic I would like to discuss. They would all moan and groan and roll their eyes. I think most of the time it wasn't because they didn't want to hear what I had to say. They moaned mostly because I would take too long to say it. So I have determined that: *We don't have to be great scholars of doctrine, but we do need to be men of action.* We can teach by doing.

A few years ago, my oldest daughter was pondering getting married and beginning a family of her own. She asked me, "Now that your children are growing up and leaving home, what do you have to look forward to?"

I don't exactly remember what my answer was at that time. I probably said something like, "I am not as old as you think I am and there is a lot to look forward to." But, her question is a very good one and I have thought about it many times since. When pondering this question there can be many items listed such as traveling, more time to read, genealogy, giving service, missionary work, writing a book, etc... Keeping with the theme of this book, which is fatherhood and the importance of family, my short answer would be, "If we have done our job correctly as parents, (if we have been men of action), we should be able to participate in many of these activities and look forward to many more wonderful times together as families."

I believe that if we haven't taken the time when the kids were younger to enjoy being together and doing stuff together, then neither they nor we will know how to enjoy being and doing stuff together later. Maybe we won't know what to do to enjoy time together. Or, sadly, we might just not enjoy time together at all.

This reminds me of a very sad story. As part of our church service as home teachers, Kevin and I would pay monthly visits to an older lady that lived not too far from our home. She lived alone and was suffering with health issues. As Kevin and I got to know her better, we learned that her health problems were very serious; she had brain cancer and was going through all of the intense treatments associated with cancer. She didn't know how effective the treatments would be and she really didn't know if she would pull through, and if she did, how much time she would have after that. The saddest thing that we learned was that she had very little contact with her two grown children. They lived in different states and were busy raising their own families.

She was all alone, relying on friends instead of family at this trying time of her life.

What I picture for the next 25 years is cultivating the family interests that have been developed over the past 25 years and planning get-togethers around those interests. One of these family interests that we have been able to enjoy is trail-riding and rock-crawling in the four-wheel-drive vehicles that the boys and I have been able to modify and work on together. I know that schedules will be busy with school, jobs and small children and the like, but at least, along with the occasional holiday, we may have an excuse to enjoy some family Jeeping trips or other fun outings such as camping or boating on some short weekend excursions.

17
Summary

In conclusion, if I were to try and use one simple analogy for fatherhood, one simple thing we could remember in order to help remind us how to be a good dad, it would be this question: Are we shepherds or are we sheep herders? Do we lead with love and quiet confidence and use a comforting voice or do we try to drive our family in the right direction with actions that may resemble a barking dog nipping at their heels?

I think most dads work hard at the important aspects of raising a family and we have an idea of the direction we want to go. As we are traveling on that path, we think or assume that those around us, especially our children, should be able to clearly see and follow that same path. As a sheep herder, our view from the back, pushing, may not be the same as the view up front. Consequently, we may suffer the same frustration as the sheep herder when some of the sheep, in all of the hustle and dust and barking and confusion, choose a different path and become separated from the direction and protection we thought we were so clearly providing.

Contrast that with the shepherd who shows the way, leads by example, knows the needs of each individual, carries the ones in need, is involved, walks side by side, and offers a soothing voice of assurance and reason.

Summary

We all want our family and home to be a protection from the wolves and other everyday temptations and dangers, a place where we will be gathered in, hugged and carried by the arms of the shepherd. As we continue on the journey of fatherhood, let us remember the example of "The Good Shepherd".

To summarize my lab or field notes from our family microcosm, here is a short list of my findings that helped me as a father.

- No other success or pursuit is as important or rewarding as being a dad.

- Your family's life will be the sum total of **your** seemingly unimportant decisions. Use the Spirit to help you.
- If you will lose yourself in the well being of your family, your joy will be endless.
- Have a backyard, use it and have fun in it. Without it, you will miss out on many opportunities for joy.
- Be involved. Along with all family members attend most if not all sporting events and functions. This will help each child feel important and a part of the family.
- All punishment should be positive, thus becoming a tool and not a barrier.
- Be involved in activities that give you the chance to instruct and teach fun things. Always teach and instruct by example. As your children learn to listen to your guidance with fun things, they

will be more likely to listen to your guidance with important things.
- Family members should be among your child's best friends. If your 17 year old daughter wants to stay home on Friday night and play Guitar Hero with Dad, well, then you better be ready to play.
- Sacrifice for your children. You may have to make some sacrifices in pursuit of "Every Parent's Dream" which is; happy teenage children making good choices.
- In sports, what happens during the game is more important than the game. Build ability and confidence, build men. Of course the same applies to girls and women's sports.
- The two A's to remember for being a Dad: Adventure and Attention. To be a builder of boys you must provide adventure. To be a father of girls you must provide attention.
- Dads can cook. If you are having a BBQ, you can cook and play at the same time.
- We don't have to be great scholars of doctrine, but we do need to be men of action. We can teach by doing. If we have been men of action, we should be able to look forward to many more wonderful times together as families.

I once heard that "Love is spelled T-I-M-E." When I look back on all that has happened over the past 25 years as a dad, sometimes I feel like it all happened too quickly. Time went by too fast. I can't do it over. If I could sum up everything I have discussed in just a few sentences it would be: Enjoy every minute of your T-I-M-E as a father. Look forward to all the little blessings of fatherhood and enjoy each moment of T-I-M-E as it is happening.

www.ingramcontent.com/pod-product-compliance
Lightning Source LLC
Chambersburg PA
CBHW051805040426
42446CB00007B/523